The Power

H*of*OPE

in Hopeless Situations

The Power
HOPE *of*
in Hopeless Situations

*The True Story of One Woman Who
Called Her Husband Back from Death*

JEANNE LINVILLE

Xulon Press

Xulon Press
2301 Lucien Way #415
Maitland, FL 32751
407.339.4217
www.xulonpress.com

Writing Consultant: Melanie Hemry
Editorial: Jenny Avery
Typesetting/Layout/Cover Design: Xulon Press
Printed in the United States of America.

ISBN-13: 9781545602171

TABLE OF CONTENTS

FOREWORD

I'VE KNOWN JEANNE LINVILLE FOR ALMOST THIRTY YEARS, and I can assure you that while she has experienced incredible supernatural events in her life, she isn't a super saint. She makes mistakes, falls down, and picks herself up just like the rest of us. I interviewed Phil and Jeanne in depth after Jeanne called him back from death and wrote their story for the *Believer's Voice of Victory*. I heard her side of their story, and I heard his.

It was incredible, and it still gives me chills.

Neither of them was a super saint—and neither of them claimed to be.

While holiness is a virtue we all should aspire to, it isn't the criteria for a miracle. The Bible's criteria for experiencing the supernatural is simple.

Just believe.

Here it is in Jesus' own words: "All things are possible for him who believes" (Mark 9:23).

If you're still certain that you couldn't walk in the supernatural without being a super saint, I suggest that you consider Peter. Peter was a bit . . . impulsive. He's the one who whipped out a sword and cut off the ear of the high priest's servant.

Yet after Jesus' crucifixion and resurrection, people were healed when his *shadow* touched them!

That's what I'm talking about. An impulsive guy who operated in miracles.

Jesus didn't pull his disciples from the top biblical scholars of the day. He didn't choose pious men who fasted and prayed night and day. He chose tax collectors, sinners, and wise guys like Peter.

He chose people who, once they believed, were tenacious and refused to give up.

Tenacious.

If there was a single word I could use to describe Jeanne Linville that would be it.

Years after losing an infant son, she was faced with an even worse situation when her husband was pronounced dead. Jeanne's tenacious faith refused to let go. Hers was the kind of bull dog faith that brought him back to life.

"Sure," you might say, "but she and Phil were pastors. Of course God would perform miracles for them."

That is a common misconception. There isn't a single scripture in the Bible to support it. Pastors have to work out their salvation with fear and trembling just like everyone else. The criteria for a pastor to experience a miracle is the same as it is for you and me.

Only believe.

There is a difference though. Pastors have to live their lives, make mistakes, fall down, and get back up in a fish bowl with everyone watching.

Jeanne Linville didn't experience the miraculous because she was a pastor's wife. It was because once she found a truth in God's Word, she refused to back down.

What does that mean to you?

It means that if Jeanne Linville can experience the miraculous, supernatural works of God in her life—so can you.

Melanie Hemry

PREFACE

Sunlight streamed through the windows of my home in Edmond, Oklahoma, casting a shimmer of expectation over empty cabinets and half-packed boxes. What might look like a mess to anyone else was remnants and tatters of my life. The process of packing would have gone faster if everything I'd wrapped in newspaper hadn't brought back a host of memories so real that they'd come to life full born, tiptoeing across the kitchen floor like old friends set on surprising me.

When you're young and life stretches before you like a ribbon of promise, full of possibility and adventure, you don't get it that the years you've been given will whip by like a racecar in the Indianapolis 500. Now that I'm a grandmother, living alone after years filled with a cacophony of noise, of constant demands and crowded spaces, the quiet still comes as a shock. But here it is 2015, and I'm packing to move to Chicago.

The tricky part about slowing down, about packing your memories into boxes, is the temptation to beat yourself up over mistakes. It's impossible to look back over a life and not cringe at some of your decisions. To beg God for do-overs. My friend's five-year-old granddaughter came home from kindergarten the other day, quoting her class motto: *If you can't make a mistake, you can't make anything.* How true. Everything I've gotten right has been built on the back of the mistakes I've made. So I refuse to dwell on the failures but rather focus on the golden, defining moments along the journey.

Looking back over the tapestry of my life, I find the single most defining moment—the one that changed me in such a profound way that I would never be the same—happened when I was five years old. In an astounding touch of supernatural power, God healed my baby sister.

That experience changed me forever. We'd been raised in church and taught about God, but witnessing Patty's healing made a profound effect on me. With my childlike faith I knew God had healed my sister. I knew God still healed, that miracles still happened. I knew God was good; nobody could ever convince me otherwise.

I knew God loved me.

It was then, as I watched my sister gain weight and start smiling at me, that I was smitten with love for God. Now years later, if anything, I loved Him more. Which was why I was packing.

Here I was at my age, still lovesick for Jesus.

I wrote this book because of Him.

I want you to understand that loving Jesus isn't a prescription for a perfect life. Hard times fall on the just and the unjust, the doubter and the trustor, the faithful and the faithless.

So, you may wonder, what's the point?

The point is that you can face those trials in defeat or with the power of God in operation. Miracles do still happen. Jesus wants to grab your hand, wrap you in His love, heal your wounds, dry your tears, and get you back on your course.

You were created with a divine destiny that no one else on earth can fill.

I know what you may be thinking. That I don't know how many mistakes you've made? How many times you've fallen? It doesn't matter. Forgive yourself! Let Jesus help you up.

And whatever else you do, never, ever give up.

Jeanne Linville

ACKNOWLEDGMENTS

COUNTLESS PEOPLE IMPACTED MY LIFE IN POSITIVE WAYS during my journey, and I am grateful to them each and every person the Lord sent my way. Some, I never met in person. Still, their books, TV shows, and meetings made a huge difference in my everyday life, especially during challenging times.

Grateful appreciation to the late Dr. Oral Roberts for his radio and television evangelistic ministries that led to my sister Patti's healing from nephritis. Witnessing this healing led me to believe God was able to perform His miracles today if we will only believe.

Deepest thanks and appreciation to Kenneth and Gloria Copeland who supported me with their prayers and love when my husband was trapped in a coma, recovering from his stroke, and dealing with gangrene. The Copelands' audio recordings on faith and healing also helped sustain me as I traveled to and from the hospital during Phil's illness. I will be forever grateful for all their faith-filled input into my life.

Sincerest thanks to Charles Capps for his mini-book *God's Creative Power Will Work for You*. I spent numerous hours reading this book aloud in Phil's hospital room when I was believing God to restore Phil's life.

Heartfelt thanks to Charles and Francis Hunter who prayed for Phil while on their ministry tour in Kansas City, Missouri. Their prayer that Phil be released from the spirit of death marked the turning point in bringing him back to life.

Grateful thanks to Sharon and the late Billy Joe Daugherty for their prayers during intense moments when Phil was facing death and for their audio music recording "A Merry Heart," which not only built our faith but also restored our joy and laughter.

Special thanks to Dr. Jean-Pierre (J. P.) Mavungu, who, while he was still a respiratory therapist, became a lifeline of spiritual support not often found in institutionalized healthcare systems. J. P. arranged for Phil to attend the seminar offered by the Hunters in Kansas City. Following this experience, God took J. P. to heaven and instructed him to pray for Phil in the neurosurgical unit. J. P.'s tangible spiritual experience confirmed my expectation that Phil would live and not die. I owe J. P. so much for all the attentions and care he provided and for his moral and spiritual support as we all watched Phil on his deathbed at Saint Luke's Hospital.

Grateful thanks to my friends and family who encouraged me to hope in God and His Word regardless of the situations I was facing.

Special thanks and appreciation to Melanie Hemry for her invaluable writing expertise as well as her friendship and prayer support.

Finally, deepest thanks to God for all He has done for my family and me. I give Him all the glory and praise, for with Him all things are possible—even raising the dead.

Now faith is the substance of things hoped for,
the evidence of things not seen.

—Hebrews 11:1

Chapter 1

THE POWER OF LOVE AND LAUGHTER

LIGHT STREAMED IN THROUGH THE WINDOWS OF THE Assembly of God Church in Hannibal, Missouri, like a benediction that Sunday morning. Even better, glorious music swept like waves through the building, buoying our souls and beckoning people to come. I corralled our four kids, all dressed in their Sunday best, and got them situated. As the new organist urged a beautiful, upbeat tempo out of the old organ, my husband, Phil Linville, beamed at me from the platform.

I had learned that being a pastor's wife required abounding patience and a whopping sense of good humor. To God's credit, He'd equipped me with both, but when I failed on the former, good humor often saved the day.

After accepting pastorates in a number of small towns over the years, we'd found Hannibal to be a restful place. The parsonage, a two-story colonial, allowed our boys, Philip and Tim, to have their own bedrooms. Our daughters, Amy and Melody, shared another.

All had been well until I'd introduced some new music to the church. Although I still loved "The Old Rugged Cross" and "Just As I Am," I wanted to mix those reverent hymns with joyful praise. That hadn't sat well with our organist. At first she showed her displeasure by showing up late to the services. Then she'd stopped attending altogether.

Now that we had a new organist, the congregation seemed excited by her presence, and as I sat in the sanctuary that morning, I prayed nothing would happen to offend her. About that time a shrill, high-pitched squeal blasted through the sound system. My ears ached the way I imagined dogs felt when hearing a high-pitched whistle. I felt like howling but plastered a smile on my face.

Phil motioned for a deacon to investigate the problem. No organ on earth could compete with that mind-numbing, unrelenting scream. Phil made a brave move and stepped to the pulpit to preach. Meanwhile the deacons checked the sound system, the speakers, tape recorders, and everything electric. Nothing. Phil stood tall, his face flushed as he tried to talk over the noise. Every few minutes it ratcheted up even louder than before.

At the back of the sanctuary, the head deacon threw up his arms in defeat. They couldn't find the problem. Phil soldiered on, but the parishioners looked anguished. I noticed the new organist's face looked pinched. *Oh Lord! Give her patience!*

Laughter, the Best Medicine

Determined not to admit defeat, Phil gave an altar call. About that time an older couple slipped out of their seats to leave. They stopped to speak to one of the deacons. "Just can't hear over that blasted noise," the man said. "I kept turning up my hearing aid, but it didn't help."

As soon as they stepped outside, the screeching stopped. The silence was deafening for a moment before everyone realized what had happened. Our sound system had picked up a frequency from the man's hearing aid and blasted it through the auditorium. Every time he turned it up, the screeching had gotten louder. In the sudden silence, someone giggled. I'm pretty sure it wasn't me.

Before long twitters and chuckles mushroomed until the entire congregation gasped with laughter.

Still laughing when we got home that afternoon, Phil and I fell into one another's arms. When we caught our breath, Phil said, "I like this town and this church so much. I'll miss it if God calls us away."

"Me too," I said, still smiling as I looked up into his handsome face. "But as long as I have you, I'll be happy."

I kept a close eye on Phil those days. He worked crazy hours, and since he'd been diagnosed with diabetes, it seemed harder for him to bounce back from the fatigue that went with the job.

When the time came to leave, we did miss Hannibal. After a respite, we took a new work in Higginsville, Missouri. What started as a Bible study had grown into a congregation, and they needed a pastor. Phil accepted the call, and one of the members offered us a place to stay until the church got established and we could find a house.

A Storm Brewing

A frigid winter wind howled the day we arrived at our temporary home. I caught a glimpse of the dilapidated old farmhouse and had to swallow my dismay. Once inside, I discovered four sparse rooms and a basement with a wood-burning stove. In the kitchen, paint had peeled off the cabinets and now lay on the floor like old, discarded party favors. A mouse darted across the counter. Roaches who'd had the run of the place scurried across the worn floor, looking for a place to hide.

Members of the congregation helped us clean and paint. Within a week, a snow storm blanketed the area. Snow drifted to twelve feet on the lane between the old house and the road. That winter went on record as the worst in history for the area. To get to my job, I shuttled from the house to my car on a borrowed tractor.

By spring Phil had found us a house in town, and we moved. The long winter seemed to have taken a toll on him. He appeared exhausted and suffered bouts of dizziness. At a business meeting one Sunday evening, I thought he looked flushed. He mumbled, and I found it hard to hear what he said.

The next morning Phil went to the doctor who diagnosed him with an inner ear infection and prescribed antibiotics. His dizziness and disorientation continued, and he slept most of the day. That evening his speech sounded slurred. On Tuesday morning we drove fifty miles to the Warrensburg hospital to have him checked.

3

Although the doctors weren't sure what was going on, they admitted him for observation.

I led the service Wednesday evening, and our oldest son, Philip, took his younger brother and sisters to visit their dad. Philip's young face was creased with worry when they returned.

"Mom, something's seriously wrong," he said. "Dad doesn't look good."

The shrill jangle of the telephone sounded ominous. "Your husband has taken a turn for the worse," the doctor explained. "He's having what we call projectile vomiting, and we're arranging for him to be transferred to a hospital in Kansas City."

Race against Time

Philip and I arrived just in time to follow the ambulance. I couldn't figure out how an inner ear infection could have morphed into something requiring a late-night ambulance ride rushing him to a bigger hospital. Except for the diabetes Phil had always been in good health. Besides, he was only thirty-nine. How serious could it be?

> "WE'RE LOSING HIM! WE'RE LOSING HIM!" PHIL'S BLOOD PRESSURE BOTTOMED OUT, AND THE CARDIAC-MONITOR ALARMS SCREAMED AS HIS HEART FLATLINED.

He seemed to have stabilized by the time we arrived in Kansas City. I got to see him for a moment before being banished to the waiting room. For three grueling hours I waited and prayed.

Although I had no idea what was happening with Phil, one of the nurses described it to me later:

> The lights flashed, and an alarm sounded a warning on Phil's cardiac monitor as his heart pattern went flat.
>
> "He's in cardiac arrest!" a nurse shouted, grabbing the defibrillator paddles. "Back!" she warned.
>
> All the nurses and doctors took a step away from the bed as she delivered four hundred volts of

electricity to Phil's chest. They watched as his heart started beating again and he took a ragged breath.

Someone arrived with his lab results. His triglycerides, which should have registered two hundred, tested a staggering forty-three hundred. A handwritten note across the report said, "This blood is like Crisco."

"We're losing him! We're losing him!"

Phil's blood pressure bottomed out, and the cardiac-monitor alarms screamed as his heart flatlined.

"Back!" the nurse warned, preparing the defibrillator paddles again.

I knew none of this as the minutes ticked by on the wall clock in the waiting room. It was three o'clock in the morning when the doctor arrived. I rushed to him.

"Did you figure out what's wrong?" I asked.

"Mrs. Linville, your husband suffered a massive brain-stem stroke. We did everything we could, but we couldn't save him. I'm sorry."

Chapter 2

DANCE OF DEATH

THE DOCTOR'S WORDS MADE NO SENSE. YOUNG MEN — thirty-nine-year-old men — didn't die from strokes. Even I knew that.

My knees buckled, but before I could fall, I grasped happy memories as though I could cling to them like a life raft in a tsunami. For an instant I was a teenager again at a Youth for Christ rally the first time I'd seen Phil. Tall and handsome, he was a leader even then, singing and playing his trombone. The summer before my senior year, and we were in a quartet together. I played piano and he sang bass. We traveled to churches and sang. Our dates consisted of going to church together, attending Youth for Christ rallies, or practicing for the quartet.

I remember watching Phil shine on the football field. He'd been torn between accepting a football scholarship and following the call to ministry. He'd chosen the latter, and we'd married soon after graduation. The next summer we'd sold everything we owned and traveled to Mexico with a group of friends to minister. We'd sung in town squares and churches and had won many people to the Lord. While we were in Mexico, I realized I was pregnant.

With a child on the way, we traveled back to Kansas where Phil found a job and we attended his home church. Our son Philip was born in 1966 — a beautiful boy weighing in at over ten pounds. Two years later we moved to Texas for Phil to attend a Bible college that specialized in training missionaries. After arriving in Dallas, we discovered that the school expected both the husband and wife to attend. I hated school and had no intention of going.

But of course I did.

The college provided a nursery on campus for the baby, so Phil and I both enrolled in classes. Phil worked in the print shop, and I became the music director's secretary. On Thursdays the school required everyone to meet a human need. The streets of Dallas—and America—were flooded with hippies, the Flower Power generation. "Flower power," a slogan used during the late 1960s and early 1970s, was the hippies' symbol of passive resistance in opposition to the Vietnam War. Wearing flowers in their hair and dressed in clothes with embroidered flowers in vibrant colors, hippies became a counterculture of drugs and psychedelic music.

In short, most of them were bombed out of their minds.

New Life

We went to parks and talked to the hippies. We gave them food and often a place to stay. We read the Bible and prayed with them until many were off drugs. For some, the results were instantaneous, but others went through horrific withdrawals. Afterward many of them became part of our music department, and we formed a Christian rock band. It was a wonderful experience, and teams traveled to Mexico and Canada to minister. I wanted to go but was pregnant again, so I stayed home and worked on papers.

On January 27, 1970, our second son, Craig Anthony, was born weighing just under ten pounds. He was so cute with his chubby cheeks and bright blue eyes that Phil and I were smitten at first sight and couldn't wait to get him home. On the day Craig and I were to be discharged, Phil went to get the car while I waited for the nurse to bring Craig. When she arrived, she didn't have him.

"Craig is a little bit jaundiced," she explained. "We're going to keep him a couple of days for observation. It's probably nothing."

Phil and I both wept as we drove home without him. We felt so empty. We visited the hospital every day, and after three days they released him to come home. At last we had our little family together. We were elated and wanted nothing more than to rock him.

Although I'd taken a break from classes, Phil was still in school and driving a cab at night. Alone with both boys, I noted the differences between them. While Philip had had a lusty cry and drank his milk like he was starving, Craig was just the opposite. His cry wasn't loud. In fact, it was so soft that we kept him beside our bed to make sure we heard him. He didn't want to eat much either. He'd eat a little bit and then fall asleep.

An Uneasy Feeling

Two weeks after he came home from the hospital, Craig stopped breathing. Thinking he must have choked, I hit him on the back, and he started breathing again. The episodes happened more and more often. I knew something was wrong, so I took him to see his pediatrician. The doctor examined Craig and declared him a healthy baby and me a nervous mother who was overreacting. Dissatisfied with that answer, I took him to four more pediatricians who all told me the same thing.

> "YOUR SON STOPPED BREATHING BECAUSE HE'S BEEN HAVING EPISODES OF CARDIAC ARREST," THE DOCTOR EXPLAINED. "IN OTHER WORDS, HIS HEART HAS BEEN STOPPING."

I knew better. Sometimes a mother just knows. He was getting weaker by the day.

Craig was six weeks old the next time he stopped breathing. As soon as we got him breathing again, we rushed him to the emergency room at Children's Medical Center. They took one look at him and put him under an oxygen tent. After running a series of tests, the pediatrician gave us the results.

"Your son stopped breathing because he's been having episodes of cardiac arrest," the doctor explained. "In other words, his heart has been stopping. He was born with a heart defect called atrioventricularis communis, which means a part of his heart didn't fuse together."

"What can you do? Will you take him to surgery?" I asked, tears streaming down my face.

"I wish that were possible. There's nothing we can do. I'm sorry to tell you that your son will die—probably within the hour."

Declaring healing scriptures over Craig, Phil and I rushed to his side. "Craig, Jesus was 'wounded for our transgressions, he was bruised for our iniquities: the chastisement of our peace was upon him, and with his stripes we are healed' (Isa. 53:5 KJV).

"'No weapon formed against you shall prosper, and every tongue which rises against you in judgment you shall condemn' (Isa. 54:17).

"'When the sun was setting, all those who had any that were sick with various diseases brought them to Him; and He laid His hands on every one of them and healed them' (Luke 4:40).

"'And the whole multitude sought to touch Him, for power went out from Him and healed them all' (Luke 6:19).

"'[Jesus] Himself bore our sins on His body on the tree, that we, having died to sins, might live for righteousness—by whose stripes you were healed' (1 Pet. 2:24).

"'Is anyone among you sick? Let him call for the elders of the church, and let them pray over him, anointing him with oil in the name of the Lord. And the prayer of faith will restore the sick, and the Lord will raise him up. And if he has committed any sins, he will be forgiven' (James 5:14–15)."

On and on we went, speaking the Word of God over our son.

Second-Guessing God's Will

A strange thing happened. Craig didn't die in an hour. He didn't die that day. He didn't die that week. Or that month.

I stayed with him night and day, praying and confessing the Word of God over him. I was beyond exhausted, but he was still alive six weeks after being admitted to the hospital. When my parents came to visit, Craig was in an incubator with tubes everywhere. He looked like a little skeleton, and my dad—who was my hero—started crying at the sight.

"Jeanne, maybe it isn't God's will to heal Craig," he said.

Had I been in my right mind, I would have explained there wasn't a single scripture in the Bible to support that theory. Jesus always healed. He never turned anyone away. But in my exhaustion and because the advice came from the most spiritual man in my life, I turned to Phil and said, "Maybe it isn't God's will to heal him."

"God," Phil prayed, "if it isn't Your will to heal Craig, then go ahead and take him."

Within five minutes our son was dead.

I was livid with anger at God, and for three months I asked Him why He hadn't healed Craig. I wept as only a mourning mother could weep when He answered, *As long as you were praying and believing, I was healing Craig. But when you stopped believing, I could do nothing more because, according to your faith, be it unto you.*

I knew the Lord was referring to Matthew 9:27–29:

> And when Jesus departed thence, two blind men followed him, crying, and saying, Thou son of David, have mercy on us.
>
> And when he was come into the house, the blind men came to him: and Jesus saith unto them, Believe ye that I am able to do this? They said unto him, Yea, Lord.
>
> Then touched he their eyes, saying, *According to your faith be it unto you* (KJV).

As Phil and I searched the Scriptures, we discovered the words we'd prayed over Craig came from the prayer of consecration Jesus prayed before going to the cross. Luke 22:41–43 describes the Mount of Olives scene:

> And He withdrew from them about a stone's throw, and He knelt down and began to pray, saying, "Father, if You are willing, remove this cup from Me; yet *not My will, but Yours be done.*" Now an angel from heaven appeared to Him, strengthening Him (NASU).

Getting It Right

There in the Garden of Gethsemane was the only time Jesus ever prayed "not My will, but Yours be done." He never prayed those words anywhere else. He never prayed them over a sick person—God had made His will about healing clear. Neither did the apostles ever pray those words over anyone who was sick. Nor did the disciples.

Although our prayer for Craig sounded spiritual, there wasn't a single time in the entire Bible where that prayer was prayed over the sick. Phil and I wept in remorse and made a vow to one another that we would never give up again. Regardless of the circumstances we faced, we would believe God's Word as our final authority.

From there my mind skipped ahead to 1983 when we were pastoring the Assembly of God church in Hannibal, Missouri. We'd been raising cocker spaniel puppies for a few years and Blondie, our dog, had given birth to a litter. One of the puppies was stillborn. That happened sometimes, and we always just buried the puppy. But this time was different.

The Lord directed me to raise the puppy from the dead.

I picked the puppy up and tore the sac off him. Then I dried him off and said, "I command life back into you in the name of Jesus!"

Nothing happened.

I quoted healing scriptures over him, the same ones I'd confessed over Craig, and more.

Nothing.

I opened his mouth and blew air into his lungs.

Nothing.

I gave him CPR.

Nothing.

This went on for several hours.

I commanded life. I quoted scriptures. I refused to quit.

He took one breath. Just one. No more.

I commanded, prayed, and confessed for another forty-five minutes. He took a second breath.

I prayed until late into the night, by which point he was breathing just fine. We knew he'd be mixed in with the other puppies, nursing by morning. We wanted to know which one I'd raised from the dead, so the kids and I painted one of his paws with red nail polish. During the night, Blondie licked very bit of that red paint off, and the next day we couldn't tell that puppy from the others.

Those memories had bombarded me like time travel, in quick succession, one after another. I was stunned to hear a nurse calling my name.

"Mrs. Linville," she said with her arm around my sagging body.

I realized I was sobbing.

"Would you like to see your husband one last time?"

Chapter 3

THE POWER OF PRAISE

I STEPPED INTO THE INTENSIVE CARE UNIT AND SAW PHIL'S body lying on the bed like a discarded glove. He looked like a shell of his former self. Empty. The nurse had removed all the tubes, wires, and IVs. He'd been disconnected from everything. He wasn't breathing. There were two red, burned circles on his chest where they'd tried shocking his heart back to life. As a pastor's wife I'd seen scenes like this once too often. Never had I imagined that it would be Phil and I locked in the dance of death so soon.

First my son and now my husband.

As grief threatened to overwhelm me, a still, small voice inside me spoke these words: *If I can raise your dog from the dead, I can raise your husband.*

In a flash I realized God may have told me to pray for that dead puppy to prepare me for this day. My faith resurrected at that very moment. Tears streaming down my face, I held my husband's cold, lifeless hand and talked to him.

"Honey, do you remember the vow we made to one another when Craig died? We agreed that no matter what the circumstances, we'd never give up again. We would stand firm on the Word of God. Well, here's the thing—the situation couldn't look worse. They said you had a brain-stem stroke and they couldn't save you. I want to remind us both that nothing is impossible with God."

Then as the Spirit brought scripture after scripture to my mind, I confessed them over my husband. "According to the Word of God, no weapon formed against you shall prosper! I refute every word spoken against you in judgment! This peace and triumph is your vindication from God!

"The Word is in my mouth and in my heart! No evil shall befall you! Nor shall any plague come near your dwelling, for God shall give His angels charge over you, to keep you in all your ways.

"In the way of righteousness is life, and in its pathway *there is no death*! I take the shield of faith and quench all the fiery darts the wicked one has sent against you! A thousand may fall at your side and ten thousand at your right hand, but no plague shall come near you! God will be with you in this time of trouble! He will help you and deliver you! With long life He will satisfy you and show you His salvation!"

Words of Faith

I declared God's Word over Phil until the room felt charged with the power of heavenly hosts. Angels had swarmed the scene, drawn by God's Holy words. Sensing their presence, I knew I wasn't alone.

Eyes blazing, I said, "In the name of Jesus, I command life back into this body!"

Nothing happened.

From across Phil's bed, the nurse watched me with sorrowful eyes.

> "IN THE NAME OF JESUS, I COMMAND LIFE BACK INTO THIS BODY!"

Ignoring her, I spoke to my husband. "Phil, if you can hear me, squeeze my hand!"

The silence was broken by a gasp. Looking up, I saw the nurse, her face ashen in shock. Before she said the words, I knew what had happened. "He squeezed *my* hand!" she said before shouting for help.

Within moments, nurses and doctors filled the room, surrounding his bed.

"Don't get your hopes up," the doctor warned later that morning.

I didn't interrupt him, but it was far too late for me to take his advice. My hope had received a jolt of resurrection power.

"Your husband was without oxygen for too long. He's in a deep coma, paralyzed from the neck down and on a respirator. He'll never recover from this state."

"My husband will be healed."

Like the nurse, he looked at me with soulful eyes. He saw a wife broken in grief and out of touch with reality. If only he'd known God's Word, he would have realized that I had touched a realm of reality he didn't know.

For the next two months, I stayed at the hospital night and day. Phil's condition remained unchanged.

Having Done All—Stand

Having taken my stand, I wasn't about to let anything move me. Not the doctor's reports. Not the coma. Not paralysis. What I needed was a nuclear bomb to drop on the enemy's camp. I needed the devil and his cohorts to run like the survivors of Hiroshima, wishing they'd never touched my husband.

I knew of such a bomb.

God's secret weapon.

Praise to God was to the devil like kryptonite to Superman. Except this power was no myth.

I thought of Abraham. God had promised him a son by Sarah, who was unable to have children. According to the Bible Abraham's body was as good as dead. Anyone looking at Phil through the eyes of sight instead of the eyes of faith realized his body was as good as dead. I opened my Bible to Romans 4:18–21:

> Against all hope, Abraham in hope believed and so became the father of many nations, just as it had been said to him, "So shall your offspring be." Without weakening in his faith, *he faced the fact that his body was as good as dead*—since he was about a hundred years old—and that Sarah's womb was also dead. Yet he did not waver through unbelief regarding the promise of God, but was strengthened in his faith and *gave glory to God*, being fully persuaded that God had power to do what he had promised (NIV).

15

The Lord Remembered

When Abraham was faced with a body as good as dead, he gave glory to God. Praise released power, and Sarah conceived a son.

> The LORD graciously remembered and visited Sarah as He had said, and the LORD did for her as He had promised. So Sarah conceived and gave birth to a son for Abraham in his old age, at the appointed time of which God had spoken to him. Abraham named his son Isaac (laughter), the son to whom Sarah gave birth. So Abraham circumcised his son Isaac when he was eight days old, just as God had commanded him. Abraham was a hundred years old when his son Isaac was born. Sarah said, "God has made me laugh; all who hear [about our good news] will laugh with me." And she said, "Who would have said to Abraham that Sarah would nurse children? For I have given birth to a son by him in his old age" (Gen. 21:1–7 AMP).

Reading about Abraham's body being filled with resurrection life that allowed him to have a son gave me a boost of faith for Phil's body—which was as good as dead. Stopping what I was doing, I praised God and gave Him glory for bringing Phil back to life and restoring his body.

I turned to Galatians 3:29: "And if you belong to Christ, then you are Abraham's descendants, heirs according to promise" (NASU). Because Phil and I were in Christ, we were the legal heirs of this great man of faith! Glory to God!

God Had a Plan

I thought about the time in ancient Israel when a vast army came against Jehoshaphat and God's people. Jehoshaphat called a fast and asked for direction from God.

> Jehoshaphat *bowed down with his face to the ground*, and all the people of Judah and Jerusalem

fell down in worship before the LORD. Then some Levites from the Kohathites and Korahites *stood up and praised the LORD, the God of Israel, with a very loud voice.*

Early in the morning they left for the Desert of Tekoa. As they set out, Jehoshaphat stood and said, "Listen to me, Judah and people of Jerusalem! Have faith in the LORD your God and you will be upheld; have faith in his prophets and you will be successful." After consulting the people, Jehoshaphat *appointed men to sing to the LORD and to praise him for the splendor of his holiness as they went out at the head of the army, saying:*

"Give thanks to the LORD, for his love endures forever."

As they began to sing and praise, the LORD set ambushes against the men of Ammon and Moab and Mount Seir who were invading Judah, and they were defeated. The Ammonites and Moabites rose up against the men from Mount Seir to destroy and annihilate them. After they finished slaughtering the men from Seir, they helped to destroy one another.

When the men of Judah came to the place that overlooks the desert and looked toward the vast army, they saw only dead bodies lying on the ground; no one had escaped. So Jehoshaphat and his men went to carry off their plunder, and they found among them a great amount of equipment and clothing and also articles of value—more than they could take away. There was so much plunder that it took three days to collect it. On the fourth day they assembled in the Valley of Berakah, where *they praised the LORD* (2 Chron. 20:18–26 NIV).

Hemmed in on Every Side

I've always found that when I'm hemmed in on every side and circumstances look hopeless, it's time to do two things: First and foremost, praise God for the victory! And second, rehearse past victories!

I went to the Bible to encourage myself in how God always came through for His people. Abraham and Jehoshaphat were under the old covenant, a covenant based on the blood of bulls and goats, yet these men experienced great victories. I was under a better covenant, one based on the precious blood of Jesus. How much more should I, God's child, experience miraculous victories?

I turned to Acts 16 and read the account of Paul and Silas. They'd been arrested, beaten, and put in prison. Things looked grim, and there didn't seem to be any way out. So what did Paul and Silas do? "About midnight Paul and Silas were *praying and singing hymns to God*, and the other prisoners were listening to them. Suddenly there was such a violent earthquake that the foundations of the prison were shaken. At once all the prison doors flew open, and everyone's chains came loose" (Acts 16:25–26 NIV).

First Thessalonians 5:18 tells us to "give thanks in all circumstances; for this is God's will for [us] in Christ Jesus" (NIV). Notice it doesn't say to give thanks *for* all things. I would never thank God for a stroke. But *in the midst* of every circumstance, it is God's will that we give thanks.

Psalm 34:1 tells us, "I will bless the Lord at all times; His praise shall continually be in my mouth" (NASU).

I praised God and worshiped Him the entire time I was in Phil's room. When I went to sleep, I praised God and thanked Him for healing Phil. When I woke the next morning, I let God know I was awake by the sound of my praise.

Chapter 4

THE POWER
OF THE BLOOD

I'D BEEN SINGING PRAISES TO GOD WHEN A DIFFERENT respiratory therapist came in to give Phil a treatment. "Hi, I'm Phil's wife, Jeanne," I said, shaking the man's hand.

"My name is J. P. Mavumga," he answered with a strong accent.

"Thank you for helping my husband. We need to keep those lungs clear because God is healing him."

"I heard much about healing as a child," J. P. said.

"Where was that?"

"My father was a preacher from the Congo who taught on healing."

"What about you?" I prodded. "Do you believe in healing?"

"I left Africa and drifted away from my father's faith," he replied with a shrug.

That night J. P. had a vivid dream. In it, Phil and another one of J. P.'s patients stood beside their hospital beds—healed. He woke with a start that woke his wife.

"What's wrong?" she asked. J. P. told her about his dream. "It was nothing," she said. "Only a dream. Go back to sleep."

J. P. drifted back to sleep and dreamed the exact same dream a second time. He woke with a strong sense that the dream had been from God. The next evening he described the dream to me.

"That's confirmation that God is answering my prayer!" I said.

Soon after that, J. P. rededicated his life to Jesus Christ. His wife made a profession of faith and was baptized. J. P. came by the room often to talk about the Bible.

Our experience with Craig wasn't the only reason I stood firm in faith over Phil's healing. I'd had my first experience witnessing supernatural healing when I was a small child. One of my earliest memories was watching my mother rock my baby sister, Patti, as she wailed. Something was wrong; even a kid could figure that out. Patti's constant cries were shrill but seemed to grow weaker as time passed. Mama took her to the doctor as many as three times in a week.

"She's seriously ill, but there's no cure for this kind of kidney ailment," Dr. Barnes confirmed as he examined Patti again. "Try to get more fluids down her."

Prayer for Patti

Our lives revolved around Patti's care. If she got too much liquid, her tiny body puffed up and swelled, causing her to cry harder. Yet the doctor insisted she needed lots of fluid to help flush out any bacteria that could accelerate the nephritis. Each evening I held Patti while Mama cooked dinner. Sometimes my brother, Floyd Jr., entertained her on a pallet while I helped Mama with chores.

One afternoon Mama turned on the television, and we settled down in the living room on our brown sofa. Mama sat on one end of the sofa, folding clean diapers and placing them in a neat stack on the coffee table. Patti lay beside me, kicking my thigh while Floyd drew funny faces outside on the sidewalk with a piece of chalk.

Mama was watching a young man named Oral Roberts preach on healing. Mama didn't so much as blink as she listened, so I listened too. People in the audience lined up to get a touch as he told everyone to expect a miracle. It was sad to watch all the sick folks gathered there. Someone had pushed a hospital bed into the tent. Other people were in wheelchairs or on crutches.

The next thing I knew, the man in the hospital bed jumped out and started weeping and yelling, "Glory!" We were transfixed by the scene.

Then Oral Roberts said, "If you or someone near you needs God to heal them, put your hand on the television as a point of contact and on the person needing healing."

"Let's do that, Mommy!" I said. "Let's touch Patti and the television while he prays!"

Mama picked up Patti and walked to the television. I stretched one hand to the baby and put one on the television while he prayed. Nothing happened. Mama patted me on the head and walked back to the sofa.

Perfect Patti

A strange thing happened that night. Mama didn't have to get up and down with the baby. She slept the entire night. The next day she retained less fluid. Each day she seemed less irritable and more playful.

The next week Dr. Barnes was amazed at her improvement. Further tests confirmed that her kidneys were working. After two more visits he released her, noting on her chart that Patti was free of the nephritis and he expected her to live a long life. As Mama prayed at dinner that night, she thanked God for the miracle of Patti's healing.

That defining moment, with a hand on Patti and a hand on the television, changed me forever. We'd been taught about God, but witnessing Patti's healing made a profound impact on me. I knew God had healed my sister. I knew God still healed, that miracles still happened. I knew God was good; nobody could ever convince me otherwise.

I knew God loved me.

It was then, as I watched my sister gain weight and start smiling at me, that I was smitten with love for Jesus. Now years later, if anything, I loved Him more.

Patti's miraculous healing was part of the reason why I refused to base my reality on the circumstances. I kept my mind on God's Word instead of the problems we faced. However, after staying with Phil night and day for two months with no outward sign of change in his condition, I knew I had to go back to my children and work to bring in some money.

Back in Higginsville, I rose early to get the children ready for school. Then I worked all day. Each evening I drove the hundred-mile round trip to spend time with Phil. Sometime after midnight I made it home.

Discouraging Words

Every day the doctors told me to prepare myself and my children for Phil's death. I stood firm, insisting that he would live and not die. At first they thought I was in shock. Later they decided I was just nuts. Phil's neurologist tried to arrange a meeting between a psychiatrist and my children. She wanted to get them the help they needed to handle Phil's death. I refused.

She was correct. I was out of touch with reality as she knew it. I understood that the doctors were giving me an accurate description of the facts. What they didn't grasp was that truth always changes facts. I didn't deny the facts of Phil's situation. I denied their right to stay that way.

When the facts threatened to overwhelm me, I remembered the story of creation in Genesis. God created the whole world and everything in it by His words. They were a creative force, and that's why I continued to speak His words over Phil.

> "Jeanne, maybe we should let him go," she said. "If he does live, the doctors all say he'll never be able to communicate or have a normal life."

Weeks passed without a single sign of improvement. Knowing I needed to boost my faith, I started listening to teaching tapes by Kenneth Copeland during the drive each evening. His non-compromising message of faith was exactly what I needed to shore up my own flagging spirit. Instead of sapping my energy, the drive helped me get through my grueling schedule.

Although Phil's prognosis remained unchanged, he stabilized enough to be moved out of the intensive care unit and into a regular hospital room. "You need to make arrangements for your husband to be placed in a nursing home," the doctor explained. "He'll remain like a vegetable for the rest of his life, never able to do anything for himself."

"God will restore him," I said.

Standing in the Gap

In addition to everything else I was doing, I also filled Phil's shoes as pastor, preaching and handling church services. I'd learned that the greatest enemy to victory wasn't the devil, the doctor's reports, or lab results. It was exhaustion that wore away at my faith, like water washing away sand. At times I felt as though my faith was eroding like the Grand Canyon. Whenever fatigue threatened to overwhelm me, I remembered Craig and told the Lord, *I'm in this for as long as it takes.*

Phil still lay in a coma on Mother's Day. I'd just finished preaching the evening service when I got a call from the hospital. "You need to get here right away," I was told. "Your husband is back in ICU—and he's dying."

Philip and I rushed back to the hospital and found Phil hovering in that thin place between life and death. Battling an infection, his temperature raged to a staggering 107 degrees. His skin sizzled to the touch. It felt like he'd been dipped into hell. If that weren't bad enough, his blood pressure had plummeted.

Sitting on the stairs outside the ICU, I felt like a child staggering to stand in the ocean. Each time I had my faith feet under me, discouragement came in like a huge wave and knocked me down so hard it felt as though I were drowning. The exhaustion alone had taken its toll, not to mention the constant stress of trying to raise four children without their father, work to provide an income, keep my faith, pray, and stand for Phil while leading services at the church.

Hazel, Phil's mother, looked at her son's lifeless body with grief etched into her face. "Jeanne, maybe we should let him go," she said. "If he does live, the doctors all say he'll never be able to communicate or have a normal life."

Strength to Stand

Her words felt like a knockout punch. I felt as though the heavyweight champion of the world had just tried to hit me out of the ring. The words hurt. "Hazel, I let the devil rob me of my son. I won't stand for him robbing me of my husband. We're going to believe what God says this time, not what the doctors say."

Staggering into the ladies' room, I didn't recognize the woman who stared back at me in the mirror. My eyes looked bruised from lack of sleep. Stress had pulled the skin tight across my bones making my face appear translucent and pale in the flickering light. Even my hair looked tired, listless, and battle worn.

I looked like I could be pronounced dead at any moment. Draped by a sheet and shoved to the morgue on a gurney. I looked like an older version of myself—that is, until I looked into my eyes. For just a moment the real me peeked out. That quick glint of light in my eyes let me know I was still alive. That I would live to fight another day. Although many people were praying, I felt as though I stood alone between my husband and a yawning grave. I teetered so close to the edge that I had to mind that I didn't tumble in myself.

Exhausted, lean from fatigue and hunger, ragged around the edges, I stood. I determined with every fiber of my spiritual authority that death couldn't have Phil. Brain damage couldn't rob him. The grave couldn't swallow him.

"In the name of Jesus," I said, my voice weak as an old woman's, "I command Phil's blood pressure to rise to normal range. I command all infection in his body be cut off from its life source. I speak to the fever, and I dismiss you. By Jesus' stripes we *were* healed. And if we *were*, then Phil is *now* healed. I release healing power to his body and to his brain. I command restoration of everything that's been stolen from him."

By the time I finished, my voice was a roar.

Passover Prayers

Back in the ICU, I opened my Bible and spoke God's Word over Phil. While he lay on his deathbed, I praised God and thanked Him for healing my husband. I remembered Passover. The children of Israel had been slaves in Egypt for four hundred years. With many signs and wonders, God demonstrated His power to Pharaoh, but he refused to let God's people go.

The last plague was the plague of death to every firstborn, from Pharaoh's house to the slave and even to the flocks and cattle. When the death angel passed over, only one thing could protect those inside.

The blood.

The blood of a sacrificial lamb that had been slain.

Using hyssop branches, the Israelites painted the lamb's blood over the doorposts of their houses. When death swept across Egypt that night, God protected all those under the blood.

So, using faith-filled words as my hyssop branch, I "painted" the doorposts of Phil's ICU room with the blood the Lamb shed for me at Calvary. Then, by faith, I put that blood over Phil's body. Over his soul and over his spirit.

Next I declared before heaven and earth—before God, His angels, and hell—that death *must pass over* Phil. That death couldn't take him. That it couldn't cross the bloodline. I sealed my declaration by taking communion. Then I released angels to minister to him.

Having done that, I slept. The next morning I woke, refreshed and ready to face a new day.

It came as no surprise to me that death sounded its retreat. Phil's blood pressure normalized. His temperature came down to normal. The infection ran for the hills.

Then, like Lazarus coming out of the tomb still wrapped in grave clothes, Phil moved his fingers. His foot twitched. His eyes opened. He was blind and couldn't see. I fell across his bed, holding him, weeping and thanking God.

Chapter 5

A STRONG SPIRIT

I LEANED OVER PHIL'S HOSPITAL BED IN THE INTENSIVE care unit and saw his eyes flutter open. Little by little his vision had returned, starting with his seeing quick flashes of light and then shapes and shadows. Today looking back at me were the stunning, intelligent green eyes of the man I loved. Seeing me, his eyes softened with the intimacy that he reserved for me alone.

He was back.

I sobbed, kissing his face, his lips, his eyes. "Oh, how I missed you!" I said, showering him with affection. I lifted each hand, kissing the fingers and the palms. I kissed the worry line between his brows. "I love you so much!"

I felt certain that no woman on earth had ever loved her husband more than I loved mine. I wanted him to feel my love in a tangible way. I wanted him to know that even though he still faced a battle to regain what he'd lost in the stroke, he wouldn't have to do it alone. The stroke had left his face pulled, paralyzed on one side. I wanted him to know that he was as handsome to me as he'd been the day we met.

He tried to speak, but it sounded like he had a mouthful of rocks. The words wouldn't form. I kissed his mouth. When he closed his eyes in frustration, I kissed his eyelids. "Everything's going to be all right," I assured him.

And it would. Together we could face anything. We were a powerhouse. With Phil at my side, I felt invincible.

It took a while for me to realize that for the first time in our marriage we were polarized by our experiences. I'd stood by his lifeless body, commanding life back into it—and had witnessed a miracle. While the battle had been long and exhausting, for me every beat of his heart and flutter of his eyelashes had been a miracle. I'd rejoiced at every milestone and every sign of life.

But while I'd fought that great battle of faith, Phil had been locked away inside some wounded part of his brain. As though from a great distance, he'd heard the doctors tell me he couldn't live. He'd heard them describe him as a vegetable. He'd heard them say that if he lived, he would never be able to do anything for himself again.

Different Kinds of Knowledge

I didn't fault the doctors. They were locked into their reality, one based on medical books and years of experience. They hadn't factored in the King of Kings, the Lion of the tribe of Judah. Their medical model didn't take into consideration the name which is above every name, the precious blood of the Lamb of God, or angels on assignments. I was thankful to the entire medical staff for providing a level of care beyond my abilities.

But those words of gloom and doom had been as dangerous to Phil's will to live as that brain-stem stroke had been to his ability to walk and talk. What he heard while locked inside the coma had wounded his spirit worse than the stroke had wounded his brain.

His reality was that one day he'd been whole and then six weeks later he'd awakened, a broken, wounded man. Every time he looked in the mirror, he saw a face pulled and drawn on one side. Having only half a normal face made him feel like only half a normal man. His body refused to obey the simplest of commands.

Nonetheless, he loved hearing how God had touched him with resurrection life. He loved the way God had proven Himself to be true and the doctors to be wrong. It strengthened him to know we hadn't made the same mistake with him that we'd made with Craig. His eyes lit up when he heard how we had let God's Word be our final authority—our only reality. He appreciated the fact that his parents had visited once a week. That my family had rallied around us and called once a day for prayer updates. That so many of his family and friends had supported him in prayer and in a hundred practical ways. But those had been our experiences.

His experience was this: At the age of thirty-nine, he couldn't walk. He couldn't talk. He couldn't feed himself. He couldn't take care of his flock. He couldn't drive. He couldn't preach. He couldn't throw a ball with his boys. He couldn't take his daughters out for a date night or talk to them about their problems.

In short, Phil Linville didn't know how to be a broken man.

Trapped and Alone

Although his mind was sound, Phil was trapped inside a body that no longer functioned. He felt alone in a way he'd never imagined a man could feel. Depression and discouragement taunted him. *You're no value to anyone. The medical expenses and hospital bills will be overwhelming. Your family would be better off without you. With you dead at least they could collect your life insurance. Welfare pays more than you'll ever be able to earn. Besides, Jeanne's strong, and Philip will help her with the younger kids. She'll make it. They'll all make it better without you. Heaven would be a million times better than this.*

As depression clouded his thinking, Phil's body responded with persistent chest pain, relieved only by nitroglycerin.

Although Phil wasn't able to speak well enough to say all these things, he told me later. But even then, when I walked into his room each evening and looked into his eyes, they told the story. A wife knows.

I also knew that just as the doctors had prescribed medicine to help his body heal, I had to find a way to heal his broken spirit.

I thought of God's promises. I knew in Proverbs 18:14 He said, "The spirit of a man sustains him in sickness, but as for a broken spirit, who can bear it?" In Proverbs 17:22 He said, "A merry heart doeth good like a medicine, but a broken spirit dries up the bones." And in Hebrews 4:12 He said, "For the word of God is living and active and sharper than any two-edged sword, and piercing as far as the division of soul and spirit, of both joints and marrow, and able to judge the thoughts and intentions of the heart."

Strength for the Spirit

For Phil to face the journey ahead, he needed a strong spirit. So when I came to spend the evenings with him, I told him story after story of the antics of our children, our dog, and members of the church. Not sad stories. I told him stories that made his face turn red as he barked with laughter, shaking his head, his eyes alight with amusement.

Then I read scripture after scripture promising healing. I knew those words were alive and would go deep into his soul and spirit, and strengthen him from within. He lay in bed and listened with eyes closed as I read.

"'The thief comes only in order to steal and kill and destroy. I came that they may have and enjoy life, and have it in abundance [to the full, till it overflows]' (John 10:10 AMP).

"'So you shall serve the LORD your God, and He will bless your bread and your water. And I will take sickness away from the midst of you' (Ex. 23:25).

"'Bless the LORD, O my soul; and all that is within me, bless His holy name! Bless the LORD, O my soul, and forget not all His benefits: who forgives all your iniquities, who heals all your diseases, who redeems your life from destruction, who crowns you with lovingkindness and tender mercies, who satisfies your mouth with good things, so that your youth is renewed like the eagle's' (Psalms 103:1–5).

"'He sent His word and healed them, and delivered them from their destructions' (Psalms 107:20).

"'Trust in the LORD with all your heart, and lean not on your own understanding; in all your ways acknowledge Him, and He shall direct your paths. Do not be wise in your own eyes; fear the LORD and depart from evil. It will be health to your flesh, and strength to your bones' (Prov. 3:5–8)."

A Higher Call

I continued reading, saying, "'My son, give attention to my words; incline your ear to my sayings. Do not let them depart from your eyes; keep them in the midst of your heart; for they are life to those who find them, and health to all their flesh' (Prov. 4:20–22).

"'But He was wounded for our transgressions, He was bruised for our iniquities; the chastisement for our peace was upon Him, and by His stripes we are healed' (Isa. 53:5).

"'For thus says the High and Lofty One Who inhabits eternity, whose name is Holy: "I dwell in the high and holy place, with him who has a contrite and humble spirit, to revive the spirit of the humble, and to revive the heart of the contrite ones. . . . I have seen his ways, and will heal him; I will also lead him, and restore comforts to him and to his mourners"' (Isa. 57:15, 18).

"'And Jesus went about all Galilee, teaching in their synagogues, preaching the gospel of the kingdom, and healing all kinds of sickness and all kinds of disease among the people' (Matt. 4:23).

"'When He had come down from the mountain, great multitudes followed Him. And behold, a leper came and worshiped Him, saying, "Lord, if You are willing, You can make me clean." Then Jesus put out His hand and touched him, saying, "I am willing; be cleansed." Immediately his leprosy was cleansed' (Matt. 8:1–3).

> "YOU'VE HEARD WHAT GOD HAS TO SAY; NOW HEAR ME. GOD CERTAINLY ISN'T THROUGH WITH YOU OR YOUR MINISTRY. HE WILL RESTORE YOU AS A PASTOR, A HUSBAND, AND A FATHER. MARK MY WORDS!"

"'Now when Jesus had come into Peter's house, He saw his wife's mother lying sick with a fever. So He touched her hand, and the fever left her. And she arose and served them' (Matt. 8:14–15).

"'When evening had come, they brought to Him many who were demon-possessed. And He cast out the spirits with a word, and healed all who were sick, that it might be fulfilled which was spoken by Isaiah the prophet, saying: "He Himself took our infirmities and bore our sicknesses"' (Matt. 8:16–17).

"'But when Jesus knew it, He withdrew from there. And great multitudes followed Him, and He healed them all' (Matt. 12:15)."

As I read, I sensed Phil's spirit come alive. It seemed as though every fiber of his being responded to the life in God's Words. When it was time for me to start the long drive home, I kissed him. Then I locked my eyes with his and spoke to his inner man.

"You've heard what God has to say; now hear me. God certainly isn't through with you or your ministry. He will restore you as a pastor, a husband, and a father. Mark my words!"

Chapter 6

A PAINFUL PROCESS

"BELIEVING IS A CONTINUOUS PROCESS BECAUSE MOST THE time we don't experience an immediate manifestation of our prayers," I told the congregation one Sunday morning. I wanted them to see past Phil's paralysis. I wanted to help them see through the eyes of faith—to see him healed. They were elated when Phil woke from his coma but dismayed that he still suffered from the effects of the stroke.

The medical staff tried to figure out how well Phil could see. They also wanted to find a way to communicate with him. Their first attempt had been to hold a blackboard in front of him with letters and words on it. When that didn't work, they placed an electronic board at the foot of his bed.

"Dad," Philip said one day, "as we go through the alphabet, squeeze my hand when you want to choose a letter." Philip's simple plan worked, and Phil began squeezing his hand when we read certain letters.

V – E – G –E – T – A –B – L – E

The first word he communicated with us was the word that he'd heard over and over while in a coma! *Vegetable!* Then as though playing charades, he made a face that said what was on his mind. *In your face, devil!*

We burst out laughing and said, "Yeah, in your face, devil!" Phil's lopsided grin gave over to laughter. He was laughing at the devil!

My man was back.

While Phil faced challenges to his recovery, we also faced challenges outside the hospital. Most of my time was spent at work or at the hospital. In addition to attending school, Philip had a part-time job. He also had the responsibility of getting his younger siblings to school and their various activities.

Since we only had one car, Philip bought an old Chevy pickup. Before long, the transmission started leaking fluid like a sieve, and after three weeks the truck died, which meant that Amy and Melody had to walk home from school.

The Great Escape

Frustrated to be stuck at home alone so much, thirteen-year-old Amy cooked up a plan of escape. "I've got an idea," she said to twelve-year-old Melody as they trudged home from school. "Let's get the key to Philip's truck and cruise around for a while!"

"Why not? There's no one at home to tell us no!"

Amy got the pickup started and backed it into the street. They'd only made it a few blocks from home when it died. This time Amy couldn't get it started again.

"We'd better get help," Amy said, her face stricken with panic. They walked to a gas station and talked to the attendant.

"Our pickup died, and it needs fluid," Amy explained.

"What kind of fluid?"

The girls looked blank. Unsure what kind it needed, they walked to a friend's house in hopes her dad could help them. Meanwhile, one of Philip's co-workers took him to meet me so that we could take my car to the hospital. "Hey, look at that old pickup on the side of the road," Philip said to his friend. "Looks just like mine and must drive like it too!" He never imagined that his little sister had gotten it running—for a few blocks.

When Philip and I got home late that evening, Amy and Melody were still up. I took one look at their long faces and knew something was wrong. That's when they confessed the great truck heist. The next evening when I relayed the story to Phil, he let me know he sympathized with their frustration.

Phil's doctors explained that when sensation returned to a paralyzed person, it always returned to the top of the body first and worked its way down to the extremities. God must have wanted those doctors to know *He* was Phil's healer, because it happened just the opposite for him. He started getting sensation in his feet and extremities first. It made a slow progression upward to the rest of his body.

A New Day

Change happened so fast that Phil's doctors moved him to the rehabilitation unit designed to prepare patients to return to normal life. Phil, impatient to get busy with his workouts, was disappointed.

He began his rehab by sitting in a chair for a few minutes at a time.

For a thirty-nine-year-old man, that was a humiliating, wimpy workout. Worse, it was exhausting. He wasn't used to being out of bed, and a few minutes felt like hours. For added humiliation, they tied him to a chair so he wouldn't fall out. And served him cold, congealed food. And talked to him like he was a toddler.

Disgusted and resentful of the demeaning situation, Phil refused to eat. When he motioned he wanted to go back to bed, the nurse said, "If you want to go back to bed, you'll have to eat your food."

He'd lost control over the simplest activities of daily living, and he hated it. Fuming with pent-up anger and frustration, Phil realized he had no control here. Nurse-zilla made all the decisions.

"This isn't a vacation," the nurse said in a no-nonsense voice. "Recovery is tedious work. If you plan to walk out of this place, it's gonna take a lot of hard work and mental toughness. I don't waste my time on whining boys who lay around feeling sorry for themselves."

Phil knew he was beat. He wanted to go home, and she was the gatekeeper. He ate the congealed food, suspecting that the next day would be worse.

He'd gotten that right.

Too Weak to Walk

Once he'd conquered sitting tied to a chair, the strong arms of an orderly and a nurse lifted him to the parallel bars. He grabbed the bars with all his strength—which wasn't much—and as soon as he attempted to put weight on his atrophied legs, they crumbled. He couldn't even pull himself off the floor.

Back in his room, he only grew madder when I tried encouraging him. I couldn't remember ever seeing him so angry and frustrated. He barked words at me that many people might not have understood. But I heard him loud and clear.

"You . . . don't . . . understand!" His green eyes flashed with fury.

I held my hand up to stop him. "You're right, I don't."

I couldn't compare my situation to his, but I'd suffered through my own Gethsemane, of sorts. I'd been ten years old, and it was my turn to wash the dishes. Mom and Dad were watching television in the living room, and the rest of the kids were playing as I banged pots and pans in the kitchen.

"THIS ISN'T A VACATION," THE NURSE SAID IN A NO-NONSENSE VOICE. "RECOVERY IS TEDIOUS WORK. IF YOU PLAN TO WALK OUT OF THIS PLACE, IT'S GONNA TAKE A LOT OF HARD WORK AND MENTAL TOUGHNESS. I DON'T WASTE MY TIME ON WHINING BOYS WHO LAY AROUND FEELING SORRY FOR THEMSELVES."

"Sounds like Jeanne's busy," Dad said, sipping his coffee.

"She doesn't like doing the dishes," Mom said, "but she has to learn that work is a part of life. I don't want her to grow up lazy."

I scraped the plates and loaded them into the kitchen sink. Now was the tricky part. Grabbing two potholders, I approached the bucket of boiling water like it was a snake. Wrapping the potholders around the handle, I picked it up and turned toward the sink.

My right foot slipped out from under me on the linoleum, and the water spilled on me. Screaming, I fell, the bucket and the rest of its contents going down with me, covering my leg and abdomen.

A World of Hurt

Bolting from the sofa, both of my parents raced to me, their faces masks of horror as I screamed in agony. Daddy tugged my jeans off and skin from my abdomen and upper thighs peeled off with them. Running to the bathroom, Daddy found sterile cotton and bandaging. Back in the kitchen, he slapped the cotton and gauze onto the burns and taped the bandage in place. He carried me, still screaming, to the car, and raced to the hospital.

"What have you done?" the doctor almost shouted at my father when he saw the bandages.

"I was trying to keep her from having any more damage," Dad said with tears brimming in his eyes.

"You made it worse!"

Dad fell into a chair and wept with his head in his hands.

I writhed in pain, screaming louder as the doctor removed the tape and bandages. Huge hunks of my skin pulled off with them. Having found someone to take care of Jimmy, Floyd, Patty, and baby Janet, Mom met us in the emergency room. I heard the doctor talk to my parents behind the white curtain.

"The burns are deep—all the way into her muscle," the doctor explained. "The burns on her abdomen are so deep that the scaring may keep her from carrying a pregnancy to term. I think she'll walk again but never without a limp."

This was long before burn units, and the small hospital in Independence, Kansas, wasn't equipped for a burn patient. They sent me home with instructions for bandage changes and a prescription for pain. The clock struck half past midnight when Dad settled me in my bed and turned off my light. Alone in the dark I said, "God, I'm asking you to heal me like You did Patti."

A Slow Process

God had done a quick work in my baby sister. That's not the way my healing manifested though. Any movement brought excruciating pain, followed by muscle spasms that built until they reached critical mass and I didn't think I'd be able stand more pain. Pain meds helped some but wore off too soon. If I took aspirin with the pain med, it helped me sleep. Because aspirin could cause bleeding and didn't mix well with my other medication, I was only allowed it in sparse doses. When the pain let up enough that I could sleep, night sweats woke me as my fever soared.

Daddy sat with me several times a day and often during the night when the pain seemed more relentless. A month after the accident, bandage changes were still horrific although the muscle spasms had diminished in severity.

"You're strong. You'll be all right," Mom said as she sat a tray of food beside my bed.

I forced myself to eat while the rest of the family chattered away at the dining table. Gritting my teeth, I stretched my right leg and tried to touch the foot of the bed. The pain was agonizing, and my bent knee refused to budge.

"What are you doing?" Daddy asked one morning when he found me in a cold sweat and obvious pain.

"I'm stretching my legs," I said between gritted teeth. "I'm not going to walk with a limp!"

"You can do it, Sunshine!" Dad said with a glint of admiration in his eyes. "Come on. Just a little farther!"

Six weeks after the accident, I went back to see the doctor. "I'm amazed at how far you can move your legs!" he said. If only he'd stopped there. "You're doing great, but don't expect too much. The scarring is so deep that your muscle tissue may never extend to its normal length. Scar tissue doesn't have the elasticity of normal tissue. Keep exercising, but don't expect it to ever be back to normal."

I don't know which was worse, stretching burned muscles or getting the doctor's negative words out of my head.

After that visit, I put my crutches in the closet and refused to use them. I started putting weight on that leg while walking around the house. When the weather was nice, I went outside and hung from the branch of a tree. The weight of my own body pulled and extended my leg. Whenever I caught myself limping or walking stooped, I stopped and made myself start over. In time I went back to school—without a limp.

While I couldn't imagine how difficult Phil's situation was, I had a glimmer of understanding and compassion.

Chapter 7

THE STEPS OF A RIGHTEOUS MAN

REHABILITATION WAS A GRUELING PROCESS. IN ADDITION to the physical therapy, Phil worked with a speech therapist, which made communication easier. One evening after he was back in his room from rehab, I asked the question that had been burning in my mind.

"What was it like to die?"

Phil took his time, enunciating each word. "It was like being suspended in time and space," he said. "I was engulfed in a sense of weightlessness. I remember expecting to see my angel come take me to the Lord. I knew it would be wonderful to be with Him."

"Did you see God?"

"Yes. I heard the Father's voice ask, 'What have you done with My Son, Jesus?' I said, 'Lord, you know!' At that moment I knew I was at the mercy of God. My confidence was that my name was written in the Book of Life. I was flooded with a deep sense of eternal peace. There were no worries. No regrets. No fear. Just peace.

"There were no thoughts of all the complicated anxieties of life here on earth. There was no consideration of bank accounts, percentages of interest, or how many members attended the church. None of that mattered at all. The only thing that mattered were eternal works, particularly those done in secret. It amazed me how very little mattered in the face of eternity."

I let him rest a few minutes and then prodded further. "What else do you remember?"

"When the body dies, our spirits are still alive and fully functional. I remember hearing you tell me to squeeze your hand," Phil explained. "I thought, *Sure! I can do that!* Even while I was in a coma and on the ventilator, I knew everything that was going on, and I heard what was said around me. I heard and understood the doctors' dire predictions. I heard what each visitor said. Some encouraged me; I wished others hadn't bothered coming."

> "I REMEMBER THINKING I'D LIKE TO ENCOURAGE OTHERS NEVER TO GIVE UP ON ANYONE WHO WAS IN A COMA. I WANTED TO URGE EVERYONE, EVEN MEDICAL PERSONNEL, TO SPEAK POSITIVE WORDS TO THE PERSON AND ASSUME HE WAS HEARING AND UNDERSTANDING EVERYTHING GOING ON AROUND HIM."

Phil Remembers

He continued sharing, his words labored but his eyes full of light.

"I loved hearing you read and quote Scripture to me. My mind was so clear that I meditated on all the Scriptures. I had a new perspective on heaven and earth. It was so real to me that I wanted to preach it. One verse in particular took on a new meaning. It was Matthew 16:26, 'For what will it profit a man if he gains the whole world, but forfeits his soul? Or what will a man give in exchange for his soul?'

"While I was in the coma, I also thought about Psalm 90:10: 'The days of our lives are seventy years; and if by reason of strength they are eighty years, yet their boast is only labor and sorrow; for it is soon cut off, and we fly away.' The psalmist was saying that life isn't very long, and we should make the most of our time on earth.

"I remember pondering Psalm 91:1, 'He that dwelleth in the secret place of the most High shall abide under the shadow of the Almighty.' I knew I was in that secret place under the shadow of the Almighty. I had a fresh revelation that God keeps those who put their trust in Him."

Phil dozed for a little while, but when he woke, he picked up where he'd left off.

"I remember thinking I'd like to encourage others never to give up on anyone who was in a coma. I wanted to urge everyone, even medical personnel, to speak positive words to the person and assume he was hearing and understanding everything going on around him.

"Every evening before you left the hospital, I heard you say, 'Phil, you're going to be totally well and fully functional as a pastor, a husband, and a father.' Those words meant everything to me. They supported me while I was locked away in the tortured loneliness of the coma. I wanted to tell you how much I loved you and the kids." He reached over and took my hand. "More than anything, I wanted to do this . . . just talk."

One evening J. P. Mavumga, our respiratory therapist friend, brought exciting news. "Charles and Francis Hunter are going to hold a healing meeting here in Kansas City!" Turning to Phil, he asked, "Would you like to go?"

"Of course I would," Phil responded. "But how can I?"

"I'm going to ask for permission to take you in a wheelchair!"

J. P. must have been very persuasive because those in authority approved the outing.

The Happy Hunters

Charles and Francis Hunter had an amazing healing ministry and were often called "the Happy Hunters." I was delighted for Phil to be touched by their faith and be prayed for by them. In addition to needing healing, he also needed a dose of their joy.

When the appointed day arrived, J. P. and I helped Phil into a wheelchair and took him to the meeting. By now it had been two-and-a-half months since he'd been in a worship service. Phil laughed and cried as we sang and praised God. I realized that as much as physical therapy was rehabilitating his body, our worship was rehabilitating his soul. He drank in the experience like a man dying of thirst.

During ministry the Hunters rebuked the spirit of death and prayed and prophesied over Phil. Charles Hunter asked him to do something he hadn't been able to do. By the time we left. Phil was able to move his leg in ways he hadn't been able to since his stroke. He also radiated joy. He'd gotten a big dose of their happiness, which was just what he needed to combat the depression that plagued him.

Over the next few weeks, I saw something incredible happen to Phil; he took his life back. His faith had been resuscitated by the Hunters, and he *believed* he was healed.

He conquered the parallel bars!

He walked!

A few short weeks after the Hunters prayed for him, Phil had improved so much that he was discharged!

Although he'd been in the hospital for three long months, the last day felt the longest to him. He was ready to leave the moment his neurologist wrote the order, but that didn't happen.

Home Again

Medication orders had to be written; a nutritionist had to meet with him about his diet; the physical therapist had to order equipment and give him discharge instructions: each discipline had to do the same thing.

Hours passed before his nurse helped him into a wheelchair for the last time. All of his caregivers gave him fond farewells. I'd driven in from Higginsville and had pulled the car to the front door. By now, Phil was exhausted but pumped about going home. The drive home took an hour, and by the time we reached Higginsville, Phil was dozing. At home, we had trouble waking him; it looked as though he was drifting back into a coma. I called an ambulance and put a call in to the doctor. The doctor returned my call and asked, "How long has it been since he's eaten?"

It had been hours! When his discharge order had been processed, dietary had stopped sending meals. In all the hubbub, no one realized he hadn't eaten, and he'd been too excited to think about food.

"Give him orange juice," the doctor ordered.

The orange juice raised his blood sugar, and Phil opened his eyes. I canceled the ambulance.

The kids were thrilled to have their dad home again; they all vied for his attention, almost tripping over themselves to be heard. Although exhausted, Phil loved every minute of it. Everyone was so excited for the whole family to be together again that no one wanted to stop the celebration.

Together Again

It was getting late, so I sent the kids to bed. When the house got quiet, I locked the doors and turned off the lights. Back in our bedroom, Phil was already asleep. Pulling back the covers, I crawled into bed and curled up next to him.

Tired as I was, I knew I'd never forget that moment. Moonlight spilled into the room, lighting his face in profile as I stared at his features. For the first time in months, I let myself remember.

I heard those words again, "Mrs. Linville, your husband suffered a massive brain-stem stroke. We did everything we could, but we couldn't save him. I'm sorry." Within seconds, I'd been drowning in an ocean of loneliness. I'd felt as though I couldn't breathe: like my heart had been amputated and I'd been put on temporary life support, knowing my life would never be the same.

I heard the nurse's words cut through the fog. "Would you like to see your husband one last time?"

I remembered the horror of seeing his lifeless body. The burn marks on his chest. The way they'd removed all tubes and IVs. The horrible realization that at thirty-eight years old, I was a widow. Left alone to raise four children.

Tears streamed down my face and soaked the pillow as I remembered the words that had changed my life: *If I can raise your dog from the dead, I can raise your husband.*

I let myself bask in the joy of remembering what it was like to watch Phil come back to life. The way his heart beat again—and how brief that victory seemed to be.

The doctor's words haunted me like specters from another dimension. *Brain dead. Coma. Death inevitable. Vegetable. Vegetable. Vegetable.*

I remembered all the weeks I'd slept on the couch because I couldn't sleep in the bed without Phil. Now I touched him. I watched him breathe. I felt his chest rise and fall.

Shoving my fist into my mouth, I tried to stop the sobs. Burying my face in the pillow, I whispered my love to Jesus. "Thank You! Oh, Lord Jesus, thank You! Thank You for the cross and the empty tomb! Thank You for paying the price for our sins. Thank You for bearing the pain of our diseases. Thank You for your faithfulness! Thank You for bringing him back to life! Thank You for bringing him out of that coma! Thank You for protecting his brain! Thank You for bringing him home! I love him so much! And I love You more than words could ever express!"

Our four children were asleep in their rooms. Phil was asleep next to me. Holy Spirit had wrapped us in a cocoon of peace. I knew we still had challenges to face, but that didn't matter. I was the happiest, most grateful woman on earth. Wrapping myself around my husband, I slept.

Chapter 8

RETAKING THE REINS

THE PHONE RANG, THE DOG BARKED, AND SOMEONE pounded on the door. "Mom! Make her stop!" Amy shouted. She'd probably caught Melody going through her things. Our big, loud, boisterous, bustling family was readjusting to a new normal. Hectic as it was, I loved every minute of it. I'd missed this—life's messy moments—during the last three months. I'd missed the kids, even their bickering.

Since they were out of school for the summer, Philip, Amy, Melody, and Tim helped take care of their father while I worked. Rising early, I prepared meals so that they could eat and feed Phil without all the prep work. In addition to working my full-time job, I still preached the church services and handled church business. Members of the congregation assisted with services, visitation, and other pastoral duties. The man who owned the building where we held services allowed us to continue using it rent free so long as we planned on purchasing it.

Phil loved sleeping in his own bed and being surrounded by his family, but he was frustrated at the slow pace of his recovery. It seemed to him that the remaining partial paralysis improved at the pace of a melting iceberg. His faith was high, and he spent hours planning what needed to be done next.

"The church hasn't made any progress on purchasing the building?" he asked one evening after I'd returned home from work.

44

"No, we've just been trying to hold everything together," I explained.

Days turned into weeks and weeks into a month, and with every passing day, Phil hated relying on his children to take care of him. More than that, he resented what he considered to be my over-protective attitude.

"Phil, come outside and look what God did for us!" I said one day. Using his cane, Phil joined me on the porch. A 1979 Toyota Celica sat in the driveway, a gift from a generous friend who knew we were limited to one car. "It's an automatic transmission! Do you want to try taking it for a spin?"

It was just the step of independence he'd been needing. It took him a while to get situated, but his face lit up like the northern lights while he cruised around town and I rode shotgun.

"If you take the Toyota out today," I said as I got ready for work the next morning, "be sure to stay in town. You don't need to be out on the highway yet."

Role Reversal

Phil's face turned red and his brows furrowed. He looked at me with such frustration and anger that I had to take a deep breath and kiss him goodbye. The tables had been turned. Now I was nurse-zilla, the woman who held him back and kept him down. I couldn't imagine how hard it must have been for him to have so many limitations, so I tried not to feel hurt. As far as I was concerned, we'd come too far to take unnecessary risks.

The good part of his frustration was that Phil felt whole. He felt so normal that his physical limitations were nothing more than a nagging reminder of the stroke. And I was the nagging wife that reminded him.

I had no idea he was plotting to break free.

Responsibility for the congregation nibbled at his sense of duty, and he wanted to regain the reins I'd taken by default. He wanted to step back into his leadership role and move the church along by taking charge of its financial obligations. The best way to do that, he figured, was to meet with the man who owned the building and hammer out a deal with him. He could have asked Philip or me to drive him, or someone in the church for that matter, but that's not what he wanted. Thrilled to be climbing back in the saddle again, he was like Frank Sinatra singing, "I did it my way!"

Convinced that my prying eyes missed nothing, he put on an act worthy of an academy award as he planned his escape. The man he wanted to meet lived in a town about fifty miles away. Phil thought it was ridiculous that I'd said he shouldn't drive on the interstate yet. He'd done fine driving around town a few times. He was determined to drive himself to the meeting in spite of my embargo against long-distance driving. He was going to show me a thing or two. In addition, he felt certain that when I found out he'd succeeded in his quest, I'd be proud of him.

I had no idea when I left for work that morning he was going to leave too.

Making a Run for It

Seeing the coast was clear, Phil limped to the car. He propped his cane against the vehicle before unlocking and opening the driver's door. Turning backwards, he let his body fall into the seat and then pulled his legs inside. After reaching out to grab his cane, he slammed the door.

Starting the car, Phil listened to the engine and thought it sounded powerful. For the first time since his stroke, *he* felt powerful and in control of his destiny. While the car warmed up, he remembered the first time he'd driven his dad's Buick.

Today felt like another milestone in his life.

Backing out of the driveway, Phil drove down the street and turned toward Interstate 70.

He merged into traffic on the interstate, happy with his progress. Turning on the radio, he tuned it to a local Christian radio station. He rolled down the window and settled in to the seat for the fifty-mile drive. Resting his elbow on the open window, he enjoyed the feel of the wind in his face. Sun shone from a clear sky, and the music lifted his soul.

It was a good day to be alive.

It was a great day to be in control of his own life.

He pictured the pleasure on my face when I realized he'd taken charge of church affairs again. The miles zipped along as he thought through his talking points with the owner and imagined driving home in triumph.

The Slow Lane

Deciding that he should avoid having to maneuver in fast traffic, Phil stayed in the right lane at fifty-five miles an hour. About thirty miles into his journey, Phil got stuck behind a large truck and missed the sign that warned drivers of construction ahead. He didn't see the warning that traffic was being rerouted around the construction—nor did he see the lowered speed limit.

He continued on at fifty-five miles an hour.

When the truck changed lanes, Phil noticed a gravel road just ahead. Knowing he was going too fast, he braked . . . too hard. The car went into a slide and then flew into the air.

> *"JESUS!"* PHIL SCREAMED, SECONDS BEFORE THE CAR FLEW INTO A DITCH AND THEN CRASHED INTO THE SIDE OF A METAL BUILDING, JUST MISSING AN I-BEAM.

"*Jesus!*" Phil screamed, seconds before the car flew into a ditch and then crashed into the side of a metal building, just missing an I-beam.

He heard the engine running and the Lord's warning, *Get out!*

It took a minute for Phil's mind to clear and then he tried to get out of the wreckage. Both doors were jammed shut. Stretching across the front seat, he kicked his weak legs upward at the driver's door with all his strength.

Nothing. The door didn't budge.

Gathering his trembling legs again, he kicked.

Nothing.

Exhausted and shaking all over, he sensed the Lord warn him again. *Get out!*

Phil kicked the door with all his strength.

The door exploded off its hinges and dropped to the ground. Grabbing his cane, he crawled out of the demolished vehicle. When he stepped outside, he sank in mud up to his knees. He was trapped and unable to move. Blood streamed from lacerations on his face as he waved his cane in the air and shouted for help.

Another Miracle

Someone heard him, and a group of men pulled him out of the mud, easing him onto solid ground. An ambulance screamed to a stop and EMTs helped him onto a stretcher.

"We've seen a lot of people die with a whole lot less damage to their cars than this," one of the men said.

Phil turned to look at the Toyota. It was a mangled mess.

As the paramedics lifted him into the ambulance, he remembered calling on the name of Jesus. That name had invoked angels to keep him safe. His error in judgment hadn't caused God to remove His protection.

As the ambulance raced toward the hospital, Phil groaned, not from pain, but from the thought of facing me.

Knowing nothing about his escapade, I answered the phone on my desk a while later without any premonition of problems.

"I'd like to speak to Jeanne Linville," someone said.

"This is she! How may I help you?"

"I'm calling from Lee's Summit Hospital. Your husband has been in an accident. He's alive and doing well, but you need to come."

"Wait . . . *what?* I'm sorry, there must be a mistake. My husband is at home."

"Is your husband's name Phil Linville?"

"Yes."

"Then there's no mistake. He was in a single car accident, and we have him here."

I felt dinged. Like I'd entered the Twilight Zone. How had Phil gotten to Lee's Summit? *Alone! Why?*

The Clash

I asked to be excused from work and then called Philip to let him know where I was going. Afterward I left for Lee's Summit, seething the whole way. By the time I reached the emergency room, I was furious.

"Phil," I said storming into his cubicle, "what were you *thinking*?"

"I wanted to get this business with the church finished," he said as his face flushed red.

"You weren't thinking about anyone except yourself!"

"I'm sorry, honey."

"The car's totaled!"

"I know. I did so well until I got here."

"I just got you back! You could have been *killed!*"

"I know."

Once the medical staff was sure he had no life-threatening injuries and was stable, they dismissed him. It was a long drive home.

We didn't speak.

He had no idea what I'd lived through. None. He'd never had to stand over my lifeless body. He'd never had to face the rest of his life without me. He'd never had to call life back into me. He'd never had to face down doctors and the devil.

Of course, I didn't understand how hard this had been on him.

But he didn't have an inkling of what I'd been through. Going and coming from Lee's Summit, I'd seen what was left of our Toyota.

He shouldn't have survived.

Phil Linville had received another miracle.

When I looked at that wreckage, I felt like I'd been dropped into the vortex of a tornado and every molecule of my being was spinning away. I needed God to pull the pieces back together.

I didn't know how many more close calls my heart could handle.

Chapter 9

DEATH STALKS AGAIN

"JEANNE, I WANT YOU TO PROMISE ME YOU'LL GO TO THE doctor and get that mole checked," my mother insisted while we cleaned the kitchen. My parents had made the trip to visit on a regular basis while Phil had been in the hospital. Now that he was home, they continued coming to lend a hand. Though I appreciated them a great deal, Mom was like a broken record, and it had begun to irritate me.

I had a mole on the inside of my right arm about the size of an eraser on the end of a pencil. It had been there for a while but had started seeping fluid. I had enough on my plate without worrying about a mole.

"Mom, I'm going to trust God about the mole," I said as I hung the dish towel on the oven handle to dry.

"Honey, your mother's right," Phil chimed in. "It keeps getting bigger, and now its leaking. Those kinds of changes to a mole are reasons to get it checked."

"After all the miracles you've experienced, I don't understand why you won't just use your faith and get into agreement with me that I'm healed!"

"You're right, God performed amazing miracles on my behalf. But He used the skills of the medical staff to keep me going until my healing manifested. There's nothing wrong about using doctors. You know that."

"All right! I'll go see the doctor. But I'm telling you right now, no matter what he says, I'm trusting God."

Phil insisted on going with me to have the mole examined. I hated taking more time off work, but between Phil and my mother, they wouldn't give it a rest.

"This isn't a simple mole," the dermatologist said. "It's melanoma, the worst and fastest growing skin cancer known to man. If we don't remove it, you'll be dead in three months. If we do remove it, the best I can offer is that it will buy you some time. I want to get you on the surgical schedule right away."

I thought about Proverbs 18:21, that "death and life are in the power of the tongue," and I knew what came out of my mouth now would set my course.

"God is my healer," I said. "My trust is in Him."

Double-Teamed

Phil called my mother as soon as we got home. They both hammered away at me with all the reasons why I should have the surgery. Either one of them was a force to be reckoned with. Together they were unstoppable.

"Oh, all right!" I said throwing my hands into the air. "I'll get the ugly thing removed if it'll make you both happy!"

"THIS ISN'T A SIMPLE MOLE," THE DERMATOLOGIST SAID. "IT'S MELANOMA, THE WORST AND FASTEST GROWING SKIN CANCER KNOWN TO MAN."

The next Thursday I was admitted to the hospital for an overnight stay. When I woke in the recovery room, a large ace bandage was wrapped around my arm where the doctor had removed the growth.

"Everything went well," the doctor explained. "I'll write you a prescription for pain pills."

"I'm not in any pain," I said. "I'd rather not take anything if I don't have to."

He instructed me to leave the dressing on my arm until he saw me at my follow-up visit.

Two weeks later I almost fainted when he removed the dressing. "What have you done to me?" I asked with tears streaming down my face. "You've mutilated me!" A huge chunk of my arm was missing almost all the way to the bone.

"We always take that much tissue to make sure we get all the cancer," the doctor explained. "Even so, Mrs. Linville, you still might die."

I took one look at Phil and realized he'd just gotten a tiny glimmer of what I'd been through with him. I wasn't dead—far from it. But I'd received what could be interpreted as a death sentence. All the color drained from Phil's face, and he looked at me as though I were fragile and might break. Okay, sure, I'd wanted him to understand why my heart couldn't handle any more close calls where he was concerned. But not this way.

Back home, I thought about all the things the doctor had said. That removing the growth would just buy me time. That I might still die. Just like in Phil's case, I wasn't disputing the facts of the situation. However, I was going to a higher authority, which was Truth.

I refused to live my life with those threats hanging over my head.

Faith versus Denial

I was well aware that from the outside faith and denial looked the same. But they were very different. *Denial* is a mental process where you know in your mind Jesus paid the price for healing on Calvary, and so you ignore the facts. That way of thinking can look a lot like faith.

So how can you know you're in faith and not denial?

Romans 10:17 says, "So then faith comes by hearing, and hearing by the Word of God." In other words, *faith* is much more than mental agreement. Faith comes by meditating on and hearing the Word of God.

I knew that if I needed to be healed, meditating on and hearing God's Word concerning *creation* wouldn't yield faith for *healing*. I also knew that for whatever problem I faced, I needed to *grow* my faith in that area by meditating on and hearing what God had to say on the subject.

Joshua 1:8 tells us, "This book of the law shall not depart out of thy mouth, but thou shalt meditate thereon day and night, that thou mayest observe to do according to all that is written therein: for then thou shalt make thy way prosperous, and then thou shalt have good success" (ASV).

Another translation says it this way: "Never stop speaking about this Instruction scroll. Recite it day and night so you can carefully obey everything written in it. Then you will accomplish your objectives and you will succeed" (CEB).

Back to the Basics

My faith was already on high alert because of the stand I'd taken for Phil. Still, I knew that the devil would like nothing more than to take us out. So I had to keep my faith alive and well. That meant I had to meditate and hear myself say what God said about my situation.

I opened my Bible and read the scriptures out loud as though the Lord were speaking directly to me:

"'The prayer of faith will save the sick, and the Lord will raise him up. And if he has committed sins, he will be forgiven' (James 5:15).

"'Whatever you ask in prayer, believing, you will receive' (Matt. 21:22).

"'Without faith it is impossible to please Him, for he who comes to God must believe that He is, and that He is a rewarder of those who diligently seek Him' (Heb. 11:6).

"According to Matthew 17:20, I activate my mustard seed of faith and say to mountains of sickness and disease in my life—including melanoma—be removed!

"According to Matthew 8:10, I have uncommon, great faith in the power of Jesus!

"According to Hebrews 11:39–40, I declare that I will not only receive a good testimony of faithfulness, but I will also receive *all* that God has promised!

"According to Hebrews 11:30, I will encircle the immovable walls in my life, and by faith those walls will fall down!

"I will not perish with those who do not believe (Heb. 11:31).

"According to 2 Corinthians 1:21, I am established and anointed by God.

"Lord, I pray as your disciples prayed in Luke 17:5. Increase my faith!

"I will not be weak in faith! According to Romans 4:19, like Abraham, I declare that my body is not dead but alive to birth the gifts and anointing God has set aside for me.

"According to Romans 10:17, my faith increases the more I hear, and I hear by the Word of God."

Getting God's Mind on the Matter

I continued reading aloud.

"Even though I go through trials, according to 1 Corinthians 10:13, You will not allow me to face anything I can't overcome!

"According to 2 Corinthians 5:7, I walk by faith and not by sight.

"According to Hebrews 11:13, I see through the eyes of faith the promise of things far off. I am persuaded of their reality.

"According to James 1:6, I come boldly before God, asking in faith for my healing. I will stand firm and not waver!

"Thank You, God, that the testing of my faith produces patience to wait for Your Word to manifest in my life (James 1:3).

"According to 1 Timothy 3:9, I hold the mystery of faith with a pure conscience.

"According to Galatians 3:26, I am a son of God because I have faith in Jesus Christ.

"According to Luke 7:50, I go in peace because my faith has saved me.

"According to James 2:17, my faith is alive!

"According to 1 Corinthians 12:9, I desire and receive the gift of faith from the Spirit of God.

"According to Acts 6:8, I do great wonders because I am full of faith.

"According to Luke 22:32, my faith will not fail!

"According to Hebrews 4:2, God's Word profits me because I mix what I've heard with faith.

"According to Jude 3, I contend for the faith that was delivered to me.

"According to Ephesians 6:16, I take the shield of faith and quench all the fiery darts of the wicked one—including melanoma!

"According to Galatians 3:13, Christ has redeemed me from the curse of the law, having become a curse for me. Because it is written, 'Cursed is everyone who hangs on a tree.'"

Days passed, and I meditated on God's promises, confessing them out loud so that I could hear myself say them. Faith took root in me, and I rested in the assurance of my healing. On the anniversary of my surgery, I got a letter from the doctor.

It was addressed to "Jeanne Linville or Survivor."

My family had been through enough, and I didn't want them to worry. So I threw the letter into the trash. Every year on the anniversary of my surgery, I got the same letter in the mail addressed to Jeanne Linville or Survivor. Every year I tossed it in the trash.

After seven years the letters stopped.

I guess they decided I wasn't going to die after all.

Chapter 10

MAINTAINING
THE VICTORY

PHIL WALKED TO THE PULPIT AND OPENED HIS BIBLE TO thunderous applause. Tears streamed down my face as we gave him a standing ovation. It looked as though the whole town had turned out to hear him.

Five-and-a-half months after Phil had suffered the brain-stem stroke and been pronounced dead, he was back in the pulpit. I wished every doctor who had predicted his death could be here now. I wished the psychiatrist who'd wanted to help us face reality was here. I wished every person who'd had a hand in his care could celebrate this milestone with us.

Phil and I had learned the hard way that life and death are in the power of the tongue. We'd always believed God had created the world through His spoken words and that He'd made us in His image. Now we understood firsthand we had the same creative power in our words that He had.

Phil's face was drawn to the side, giving him a lopsided grin. And he was still working on speaking with clarity. While at times his recovery had seemed slow, less than six months from death to back in the pulpit was an amazing feat of God! How faithful He'd been! How true His promises had proven to be!

In time, the church in Higginsville purchased a parsonage. I enjoyed taking Phil a glass of iced tea on Saturdays when he stood outside on a ladder hammering nails. Knowing this was the life I'd almost missed, I loved watching him.

Looking back, I saw myself standing at a crossroads beside his dead body. It could have gone either way.

The Lord says in Hosea 4:6, "My people are destroyed for a lack of knowledge." That's why we'd lost Craig—we'd lacked the knowledge of God's will and His Word. Had we not learned the truth of God's Word back then, I would've been facing an alternate reality now.

For Phil, fighting his way back from the effects of the stroke had been difficult. God's best isn't always the easiest path. Taking a stand on God's Word when every shred of natural evidence declared me a fool hadn't been a picnic for me either. But watching Phil in the pulpit gave me chills. Seeing him discussing college and the future with Philip was worth it all. Hearing him talk to his daughters about boys made my breath catch. Knowing he was outside pitching a ball with Tim was priceless.

The Moments That Matter

How could I measure life, if not for those moments? The struggles we'd both gone through to get to this place were nothing compared to the joy of basking in the moments we would have once taken for granted.

Of course, life was still not without its challenges. After the initial rush of excitement over Phil's return to the pulpit, church attendance dwindled to almost nothing. While everyone had been thrilled to hear his experience, they'd been less than excited about following a pastor recovering from a stroke. In time we left Higginsville and followed the leading of the Lord to different places.

Even so, my opinion hadn't changed. I didn't care where we lived—so long as Phil was by my side.

As news of Phil's miracle spread, many opportunities came our way. In January of 1990, our story was featured in Kenneth Copeland's magazine, *Believer's Voice of Victory*. The following year the story was featured on their television broadcast. Our story was also published in *Voice*, the magazine of the Full Gospel Business Men's Fellowship, and in *Christian Family*. We spoke at Full Gospel Business Men's Fellowship meetings, and I spoke at Women's Aglow.

These were the upsides of our testimony. The hard part, of course, was that to have a testimony, there has to be a test. Phil's stroke and death had tested everything in us. Because of the test we learned to love Galatians 6:9: "And let us not grow weary while doing good, for in due season we shall reap if we do not lose heart."

There were so many times we could have fainted with fatigue and given up. That's what the enemy had wanted us to do all along. He'd wanted us to get so tired that we'd just give up—which was what had cost us Craig's life. In our exhaustion we'd fainted. We'd flinched. We'd given up.

While the battle for Phil's life had been a tough test, now we were reaping wonderful rewards. We'd wept for a season, but now we had joy every morning. The things that had bugged us before didn't bother us as much. We had a new appreciation for life and had learned to celebrate small victories.

God's Plan

After one of our moves, I accepted a new job and was ushered into the office of the president of the company, David High. As he discussed my duties, my attention kept being pulled like a magnet to a photograph of a beautiful Asian girl on his credenza. When my new boss asked if I had any questions, I did, but it wasn't about the job.

"Who is that girl?" I asked pointing at the picture.

"That's my adopted daughter, Melea. Why do you ask?"

New boss or not, I decided to be honest about the overwhelming impression I'd gotten as soon as I saw the picture.

"I think she's supposed to marry my son, Philip!"

"Really? Where is your son?"

"He's away at college."

"Well, let's see if that's God's plan."

David High, it turned out, was a Christian, and he wanted to know if God had a plan regarding our children as well. The next time Philip came home from college, we organized a picnic with both families.

Not only did Philip and Melea hit it off, they married the following year.

I had a whole new appreciation for the wisdom of King Solomon. He said, "So I commend the enjoyment of life, because there is nothing better for a person under the sun than to eat and drink and be glad. Then joy will accompany them in their toil all the days of the life God has given them under the sun" (Eccles. 8:15 NIV).

Wounded Warrior

It seemed to me that I'd come through Phil's death-to-life experience with more joy and stronger faith than ever before. In fact, the whole family seemed stronger. And yet, there was still a shadow in Phil's eyes. A wound in his soul that hadn't been healed. Back then we didn't have prayer teams specializing in trauma prayer. I know now that would have helped him so much.

We didn't know it at the time, but Higginsville marked the end of Phil's life as a full-time pastor. With me as the primary breadwinner, Phil spiraled into depression. He'd never been depressed before the stroke. He'd been happy and upbeat. A fun person. But as the years passed, I saw less of that man. I was believing God for a full restoration of everything he'd lost, including his crooked smile and the call on his life.

The thing that concerned me the most was what God says in Proverbs 29:18: "Where there is no vision, the people perish." Phil's vision for his life had been to be a pastor. Without a new vision from God, I didn't know what would happen to him. I was dancing as fast as I could, trying to earn a living and pay the bills, be there for our kids, and love and support Phil. More than anything, I was praying and believing for his full restoration. He'd lost his vision and then his hope.

The more he spiraled into depression, the more he lashed out at me. On an intellectual level, I knew I wasn't the source of his frustration. But that didn't keep me from feeling hurt, rejected, and unappreciated at times.

THE POWER OF HOPE IN HOPELESS SITUATIONS

Death Strikes Back

A frigid north wind whipped across Saginaw, Texas, one Friday morning in 1997. We'd moved to Texas to be a part of Kenneth Copeland Ministries, where Melody worked. Phil had gone to Coffeyville, Kansas, to be with his mother who'd just been diagnosed with cancer. Melody was still getting ready for work when I put on my coat and gloves. "Dee Dee, I'm going to start your car and get it warming," I said.

"Thanks, Mom!"

I stepped into the garage, still filled with unpacked boxes. Phil and I drove an old Chevette with cardboard on the floor to keep out the rain and snow. Melody drove a nice Eagle Talon. I didn't know how she'd gotten out of the car when she parked it, but I felt certain I couldn't squeeze past boxes and get in on the driver's side.

Looking at the mess, I decided to put her car in neutral and push it out of the garage before trying to start it. Working my way past stacks of boxes in high heels was a feat, but I climbed in through the passenger door and put the car in neutral. When I made my way to the front of the car and pushed, it moved *fast!*

I didn't realize the garage was on an incline.

I watched in horror as Melody's nice car rolled down the incline. *It's going to crash!*

I ran to the back of the car to try and stop it—but that didn't work. The car pushed me backwards all the way to the street! My high heels went out from under me, and I fell on my back with a jarring thud.

The back passenger tire rolled over me, stopping on my chest.

Heart Cry to God

I tried to pray, "Jesus, help me!" but I couldn't breathe. I had the weight of the car on my chest. Just then the craziest thought came to me.

Reach up and push the car off!

Shaking from the trauma, I lifted my arms and pushed.

The car lifted off me!

Not for an instant did I harbor the illusion that I'd lifted that car off my chest. The moment it moved, I knew an angel was lifting it.

60

Still having trouble breathing, I struggled to my feet. "By His stripes I am healed," I croaked. "He healed all my diseases. No weapon formed against me shall prosper."

I stumbled into the house where Melody took one look at me and screamed. "Mom! What happened?"

"The car ran over me!" I gasped.

She called her boss at Kenneth Copeland Ministries and told them what had happened and that she was taking me to the emergency room. They shut down the office to pray.

The emergency room doctor rushed me to x-ray. After all the results came back, he looked stunned. "You should have died," he said. "But there are no broken bones, cracked ribs, or punctured lungs. I'm prescribing pain medication because you'll be in extreme pain for several weeks. Don't plan on going back to work for a while."

Melody called Amy, who lived in Oklahoma, and she rushed to Texas to take care of me. The accident happened on Friday, and the pain was off the charts that day and the next. But by Sunday the pain was gone, and I was fine. I sent Amy home and went back to work on Monday.

God is amazing.

Chapter 11

JOURNEY OF FAITH

Ten years after Phil's stroke, we were empty nesters and back in Oklahoma when I came home after a long day at work. Phil was depressed and frustrated and said words that struck me to the core of my being.

"I wish you would've just let me die!"

Being stabbed with a dozen knives wouldn't have hurt as bad as those words wounded me. I'd loved him with everything I had. I'd called him back from the grave. I'd watched him celebrate the milestones in our children's lives. He would have preferred to miss all that? I vibrated with emotional pain.

"Well, then I wish I had too!" I said. "You wish I would've let you die? I won't force my faith on you ever again! Do as you wish!"

We walked around the house in a cold war.

A week later one of his feet became infected. The doctor suspected it might have been caused by a scratch or a bug bite. In the past I would have prayed over his foot and taken authority over the infection. But we were each still locked in self-pity. I figured if he wanted me to pray he could ask. Or pray himself.

I was done.

Within a short period of time, his foot was gangrenous. Two toes were black with no pink skin. There was a black spot the size of a golf ball on the top of his foot. His big toe had a black area, and there was another on the sole of his foot.

Even then we were polarized—Phil in his depression and me in my self-pity.

"What should I do about this?" Phil asked.

Still vibrating with emotional pain, I didn't offer to pray. "I'm going to work," I said. "If you want to go to the doctor, ask David to drive you."

I was at my desk that afternoon when Phil called. The doctor had admitted him to the hospital. "He said that if I don't have my foot amputated tomorrow, I'll die," Phil said.

"Let me know what you want me to believe God for, for you," I said.

The Word of the Lord

As soon as we got off the phone, the Lord spoke to me: *I know you're weary and tired of dealing with his depression. But you haven't seen the kind of depression he'll be in if they amputate his foot. It will kill him.*

I grabbed my purse and went to talk to my boss. "Phil's in the hospital, and I have to go to him," I explained. "I won't be back until he's home."

When I got to the hospital, I told Phil what God had said. He knew he was depressed. He wasn't in denial about that, but he hadn't considered how much more depressed he would be with his foot amputated.

"What if I don't have it amputated and it kills me?"

"If it kills you, I'll call you back to life again!"

I saw a spark of humor flash through his eyes. Calling him back to life had been what had brought on our cold war. If he really wanted to die, this was his opportunity to admit it.

"That's a plan," he said.

A while later the nurse came in, and I watched her debride the wound. We looked at his poor, pathetic foot, black with gangrene. Phil and I weren't ignorant. We understood the power of our words. As soon as we'd spoken death over Phil's situation, it had taken root.

An infection wasn't what had set this in motion.

Our words had allowed it.

To be more specific, our words had been a result of a lethal combination—his depression and my pity party. Phil's depression was an expression of his own pity party.

We *knew better*. We both understood it had been self-pity, murmuring, and complaining that had caused an entire generation of Israelites to die in the wilderness.

Facing Facts

My self-pity and Phil's murmuring and complaining had removed the canopy of God's blessing. Our words had allowed death to take root.

Our first mistake had been not taking our thoughts captive. Second Corinthians 10:5 tells us how to handle our thoughts: "We destroy arguments and every lofty opinion raised against the knowledge of God, and take every thought captive to obey Christ" (ESV).

> "LADY, I KNOW WHAT THE BIBLE SAYS. IT SAYS IF YOUR FOOT OFFENDS YOU, CUT IT OFF! THIS MAN'S FOOT OFFENDS HIM!"

We'd failed to rein in our runaway thoughts by letting them race along in their pity parties. The Bible was clear about how we were to focus our thoughts:

> Finally, brethren, whatsoever things are true, whatsoever things are honest, whatsoever things are just, whatsoever things are pure, whatsoever things are lovely, whatsoever things are of good report; if there be any virtue, and if there be any praise, *think on these things* (Phil. 4:8 KJV).

The second mistake we'd made was speaking those wrong thoughts. Proverbs 13:3 says, "Those who guard their lips preserve their lives, but those who speak rashly will come to ruin" (NIV).

We'd allowed self-pity to take root in our hearts, and we'd failed to take our thoughts captive. Then we'd spoken rash, wrong words that had brought ruin. In Phil's case our words had brought gangrene.

We repented.

"I'm going to fast and pray," I told Phil. "And I'm going to stay with you tonight."

If It Offends You

I knew the long night would offer many opportunities for fear, and I didn't want to leave Phil alone. The next morning I went downstairs for breakfast. When I returned to Phil's room, the surgeon was unwrapping his foot, and another doctor stood watching.

"Mrs. Linville, when are you going to do something about this foot?" the surgeon asked. His attitude was antagonistic and hostile.

"I am doing something about it. I'm praying and believing God to heal it."

"Lady, I know what the Bible says. It says if your foot offends you, cut it off! This man's foot offends him!"

"I rebuke you in the name of Jesus!" I said looking right at him. "Get out of this room! I never want to see you again!"

I fired him. Phil stayed in the hospital that day as the nurses continued to clean and debride the wounds. The next morning we were given a letter from the surgeon. He said he was resigning from Phil's case because he didn't want to be a part of his demise.

They discharged him with strict instructions. "You must be on strict bed rest," they told him. "Don't get up for any reason. If you get up, the blood poison will go to your heart and kill you."

We prayed together, agreeing that his foot was healed by Jesus' stripes and that he would live and not die. After I got him home, Phil wasn't sure what to do. "Should I stay in bed?"

"Let's think this through," I said. I opened the New International Version to Mark 11:24 and read it: "'Therefore I tell you, whatever you ask for in prayer, believe that you have received it, and it will be yours.' According to that verse, you have to believe you receive your answer before it will manifest. Now let's look at First John 5:14–15."

I turned to those verses and read them out loud.

Finding Our Footing in Faith

"Now this is the confidence that we have in Him, that if we ask anything according to His will, He hears us. And if we know that He hears us, whatever we ask, we know that we have the petitions that we have asked of Him."

We both knew those scriptures, but we needed the assurance of meditating on them now. "According to the Bible, we must believe we've received the answer before it will appear. Since we've prayed and believed for your healing, I suggest you get up and get dressed and go on about your life. I also think you need medicine, and that's what God's Word is. So I'm going to play healing scriptures and praise and worship around the clock."

In all honesty, if I'd been living by sight, I would have been scared out of my mind. In the natural, things looked touch and go. Phil was fading in and out, and he didn't look good.

That week happened to be when Kenneth and Gloria Copeland were hosting the Southwest Believer's Convention in Fort Worth. I put a mattress in the back of our van and drove Phil to the convention. I got him into a wheelchair and rolled him down front. Both Kenneth and Gloria prayed for him, and he started improving from that moment.

Back home, we got a call from Marlene Wiley. She'd been a nurse in Germany during World War II and knew a thing or two about treating gangrene. She'd heard about us through Kenneth Copeland Ministries and called to help. She asked me if I knew how to debride his wounds. I'd watched the nurses enough that I knew I could do it. She told me to debride the wounds and apply a charcoal poultice twice a day. Then she taught me how to make the poultice.

An Old Remedy

She had me go to the health food store and buy a little bottle of powdered charcoal, local raw honey, and wheat germ. Then she had me mix in a glass dish just enough raw honey with the powdered charcoal to make a paste. Next she had me mix in wheat germ to give the paste consistency when I mixed the ingredients together.

Twice a day I debrided the gangrenous wounds. Then I applied the poultice to them and wrapped his foot with gauze. Within a month his entire foot was pink and healthy except for the tips of two toes. One morning those two tiny tips fell off and Phil laughed with delight, happy to see the last of the gangrene. Losing the tips of those toes didn't interfere with his ability to walk. He never missed them.

Phil was thrilled to have both feet when he walked each of his daughters down the aisle.

Chapter 12

LOOKING BACK

WITH EACH PASSING YEAR I REALIZED THAT GOD'S IDEA of restoration was much bigger than mine. With every milestone in our lives—our children's weddings and the birth of our grandchildren—I rejoiced because Phil hadn't missed them.

One of the biggest disappointments we'd faced had been how our Bible college ended. Ours was a school that specialized in preparing and sending out missionaries whom they supported. In 1972, having finished our classwork, we'd been getting ready to graduate. The last step in the process was going to Toronto, Canada, to do our student teaching. Following that, the school was sending us to Africa and would support us while we were there.

Phil and I sold all of our furniture. We left for Canada with a baby bed, a hot plate, a mini refrigerator, and two small children. Philip was five, and Amy was a few months old. We left Dallas on a frigid January morning and started the long drive to Toronto. Along the way we stopped in Kansas to say goodbye to our families. It was a heart-rending experience because we didn't ever expect to see our grandparents again.

After tearful goodbyes we headed north. In New York we drove into a blizzard. The wind-whipped snow was so thick that we couldn't see the car ahead of us. Cars and trucks were wrecked along both sides of the road. We couldn't see to drive—but didn't dare stop. It was a white-knuckle journey, and we had to trust God for every mile. We crept along and made it to Canada.

The school had purchased an old convent where we lived. Everyone ate in the main cafeteria, and we worked in the school. We'd been there several months when I realized I was pregnant again.

We were a long way from the school's main campus in Dallas, but rumors of problems reached us in Canada. We didn't have any idea what was happening until it was over. The president of the school had had an affair. The whole thing had been exposed, and in the aftermath the school was closed.

Stranded

All the students were leaving. There were no funds to send any of us home—much less to Africa. We were speechless and in shock. We couldn't believe it. We'd sacrificed so much and were so close to fulfilling the call of God on our lives. Now we were stuck, penniless, in Canada. We had two small children, and I was pregnant with a third. We had no home, no furniture, no job, and no insurance. Our car had broken down after the long drive to Toronto.

Our families helped us get home and pick up the pieces of our lives. I gave birth to Melody, and Phil worked a secular job for a while. In time, he was asked to pastor a small church, and that began the happy years we'd spent in a series of small churches. In 1976, our son Timothy was born.

The way our school had closed and the way it had changed the course of our lives had been a huge emotional blow for both of us. But it hit Phil hardest. It had been his call and his career. While that had been a big disappointment, it was old news.

We had no idea how serious God was about giving us the desires of our hearts until He resurrected that dream on a smaller scale. In 1998—a year after Phil had been healed of gangrene— Pastors Kelly and Althea Nwaelleh invited us to teach in their Bible school for six weeks in Africa. In addition to leading the school, they pastored The Living Church in Aba, Abia State, Nigeria.

Things were so dangerous in Nigeria at that time that when we applied for a visa, it was denied. There had been so many kidnappings and murders, the state department determined that Nigeria wasn't a safe place for Americans to travel. The crimes had been perpetrated by men dressed as soldiers.

Confident that God would protect us, we continued to apply. The State Department finally granted us a visa, along with a letter discouraging us from going. We were warned, "If you go, you're on your own. Whatever you do, don't let anyone take your passport."

A Long Way to Africa

We flew into Port Harcourt, a bustling city nestled alongside the Bonny River. Although it was January, a sweltering heat steamed the makeup off my face as we stepped off the plane. Althea met us, and we left the airport by taxi for the drive to Aba.

We were just about to drive through the gate when four men dressed as soldiers blocked our way. They held machine guns.

"Just pray! Just pray!" Althea warned.

We'd been warned never to say that we'd come to the country as preachers, evangelists, or missionaries. Our answer to such questions was that we were visiting friends. Since Kelly and Althea were our friends, we didn't have any trouble staying with that response.

TWENTY MINUTES PASSED, AND THE MEN MOTIONED FOR PHIL TO ROLL DOWN HIS WINDOW. WHEN HE DID, THEY SHOVED A MACHINE GUN THROUGH THE WINDOW AND POINTED IT AT US. "GIVE US YOUR PASSPORTS!" THEY SHOUTED.

The men interrogated Althea in the harshest of terms. Over and over she insisted that we were friends who'd come to visit. They continued to badger her, the tension escalating with each passing minute.

"Give us their passports!" the men demanded.

"No, they cannot give them to you," Althea insisted.

Twenty minutes passed, and the men motioned for Phil to roll down his window. When he did, they shoved a machine gun through the window and pointed it at us. "Give us your passports!" they shouted.

It became clear to us all that they weren't going to relent. "We don't have a choice," I told Phil. We pulled out our passports, knowing the men planned on stealing them—and kidnapping us, or worse.

As we handed the men our passports, I looked the leader right in the eyes and prayed in tongues in a loud voice. I spoke with a boldness that wasn't me.

The man listened to what I said, his eyes wide with fright.

Then he threw our passports back into the car and shouted, "Get out of here! Get out!"

As we drove away, I sobbed with relief.

I've always wondered what the Lord had me say that scared them so much. It's one of the questions I'll ask in heaven.

Feeding Hungry Souls

The rest of our trip to Aba was uneventful, although the roads, which were dirt and gravel, had potholes so large that a car could fall into one and be swallowed. The other thing I noticed was that the cars were ancient.

Kelly and Althea put us up in a nice hotel. We were up early each day and taught our first class at six in the morning. We taught another class at noon, one around five, and the last one late evening. Phil and I had never experienced people so hungry for the Word of God. They couldn't get enough. In addition to ministering at the school, we went house to house praying for people and ministering to them.

Phil and I were so happy that the weeks flew by.

The only problem was, whenever Phil was teaching, preaching, or ministering, he was on top of the world. But as soon as he stepped out of that role, he slipped into a depression that bordered on despair.

If there had been a way for me to fix his emotional and mental state, I would have. But while we can use our faith and believe for other people, we cannot overrule their will. Nor will God.

I could pray for him. I could talk to him. I could encourage him. But I couldn't take his thoughts captive for him. There are some things no one can do for us. It reminds me of a sign my friend saw in Paris that read "God doesn't have any grandchildren."

That saying is true. None of us get grandfathered into the kingdom of heaven because our parents believed. We have to make that choice on our own. And once we become Christians, we may be influenced by apostles, prophets, pastors, evangelists, and teachers who open the Word of God to us. But the choices we make each and every day are our choices alone.

Taking Thoughts Captive

Every decision we make is first filtered through our thoughts. If we don't take those thoughts captive, in time they will become actions. I don't think the devil can get most Christians to take a giant leap toward darkness. But we can be influenced, one small, uncaptured thought at a time. Then we take one small step in the wrong direction, followed by another, until we don't know how we got ourselves into such a mess. We've all done it. But some of us catch ourselves—and our thoughts—sooner than others.

Back home from Africa, I rejoiced that God had restored to us something we thought had been lost forever. Phil, on the other hand, slipped into a deeper depression. Instead of rejoicing that God had let him teach for six weeks in Africa, he was embittered about the years of ministry he'd missed. Instead of rejoicing and thanking God for every moment of every day he was now experiencing, he rehearsed everything he'd lost.

I saw his downward spiral and was powerless to stop it.

Instead of turning to the Lord or me for comfort, his self-pity caused him to turn to vices that I won't name.

Long story short, in 1999 we divorced.

In an effort at total transparency, I would say this. We never stopped loving each other. He was the great love of my life, and I know I was his. I don't believe he ever gave up on God. Although he took his frustrations out on me, I don't believe he ever gave up on me—or even on us.

Phil gave up on himself.

All because he stopped taking his thoughts captive.

The Danger of Being Ungrateful

Phil reminded me of the Israelites who'd been slaves in Egypt. God had brought them out of slavery, but instead of being grateful, they whined and complained about what they missed from Egypt. In spite of seeing God perform incredible miracles on their behalf, they griped and murmured.

Phil did the same thing. God had performed an astounding miracle on his behalf. But instead of living a life of gratitude, he acted like it wasn't good enough. He griped and complained and felt sorry for himself until his heart grew bitter.

The divorce was like having my soul torn in two. But it was easier than watching him destroy himself little by little and my being unable to do anything to stop it.

In 2003, Phil suffered a heart attack and was rushed to the hospital. I was with him in the hours leading up to his death. While that time with him was hard, it was nothing compared to the agony of the last few years of our marriage.

This time I knew he was ready to go, and we were ready to let him. I knew the moment he passed away, he was in a new body, laughing with joy. He was with Craig and our parents and our loved ones who'd gone on ahead.

Good Reason

The question I've asked myself a million times over the years is, Should I have called Phil back to life that fateful day? If I had it to do over, would I call him back again?

I must say, there are valid points on each side of the argument. And I'm not too prideful to admit when I make a mistake. I've made plenty. I'm so grateful for Calvary.

But here's the honest truth: *I would do it again.*

I'm not sorry I called him back.

There are a lot of reasons why, but I'll share a few. First and foremost, Phil lived a fruitful eighteen years after I called him back to life. Our children had been young at the time, and he got to watch them grow up. He walked his daughters down the aisle. He got to know most of our grandchildren. Despite the depression that gripped him in his later years, he had many happy times in those eighteen years.

So for him, I would do it again, even knowing what the outcome would be.

But I would do it again for us. For Philip, Amy, Melody, and Tim. For me.

Yes, it was hard for us to watch him slide into depression and become self-destructive. But I know this: we would have all been so much more devastated to have lost him at thirty-nine.

What Phil didn't grasp was that *we needed him*.

He was so busy looking for a pulpit that he overlooked his flock—*us*.

He was called to go to the world. He didn't realize that he was our world.

EPILOGUE

I REMEMBER PHIL AND OUR LIVES TOGETHER WITH JOY. You may wonder how. It's because I have such an awareness of heaven. I believe the moment he stepped onto the other side, every misconception was gone. He understood what he'd been given and what he'd missed in life. I also know he somehow understood that truth without being grieved.

Sorrow was over.

Depression banished forever.

I know Phil is more alive right now than I've ever known him to be.

I'm grateful for all the years God added to his life—but that gratitude is nothing compared to what we have ahead of us. Just imagine, an eternity of serving and worshiping the Lord without sickness or sadness or loss.

The reason I have joy today is that I know this story isn't over.

The good part hasn't begun

When you're young and life stretches before you like a ribbon of promise, full of expectation and adventure, you don't get it that the years you've been given will whip by like a racecar in the Indianapolis 500. Now that I'm a great-grandmother, living alone after years filled with a cacophony of noise, of constant demands and crowded spaces, the quiet still comes as a shock.

The tricky part about slowing down, about packing your memories into boxes, is the temptation to beat yourself up over mistakes. It's impossible to look back over a life and not cringe at some of your decisions. To beg God for do-overs. My friend's five-year-old granddaughter came home from kindergarten the other day quoting her class motto: *If you can't make a mistake, you can't make anything.* How true. Everything I've gotten right has been built on the back of the mistakes I've made. So I refuse to dwell on the failures but rather focus on the golden, defining moments along the journey.

Looking back over the tapestry of my life, the single most defining moment—the one that changed me in such a profound way that I would never be the same—happened when I was three years old. That's when I fell in love with Jesus.

I love Him as much today as I did then.

I hope you've gleaned something from my story. I pray it gives you the boldness to stand firm and trust God at His Word. In the back of this book, I've included personal confessions for healing, along with scriptures promising healing.

But there's one other thing I want to add about healing.

The mistake most people make is thinking that if their healing doesn't manifest at once, it wasn't God's will to heal them. Nothing is further from the truth. That lie has been perpetrated by the devil for eons, but there isn't a single verse in the Bible to support it.

Don't get me wrong, instant miracles do occur, but they aren't very common. I'm not sure why, maybe because we're steeped in so much doubt and unbelief. But for whatever reason, most miracles happen over time. One such miracle even happened in Jesus' ministry:

> They came to Bethsaida, and some people brought a blind man and begged Jesus to touch him. He took the blind man by the hand and led him outside the village. When he had spit on the man's eyes and put his hands on him, Jesus asked, "Do you see anything?"
>
> He looked up and said, "I see people; they look like trees walking around."
>
> Once more Jesus put his hands on the man's eyes. Then his eyes were opened, his sight was restored, and he saw everything clearly (Mark 8:23–25 NIV).

In my life and the life of my family, many major miracles took several years to manifest. Sure, we received our answer when we prayed, but that wasn't when the manifestation occurred.

So don't faint. Don't say, "Well, maybe it wasn't God's will."

I've taken that road, and you don't want to do it.

When you need a miracle, turn to Jesus.

He's still the Miracle Worker today.

And once you've taken your stand—keep standing.

Never Quit. Never give up.

Appendix A

SCRIPTURE CONFESSIONS FOR HEALING

Isaiah 54:17
No weapon formed against me prospers, and every tongue that rises against me in judgment, I condemn.

Romans 10:8 (KJV)
The Word is nigh me, in my heart and in my mouth.

Psalms 91:10–11
Because I have made the LORD my refuge and my dwelling place, no evil shall befall me, nor shall any plague come near my dwelling.

Proverbs 12:28
In my pathway is life and not death.

Ephesians 6:16 (KJV)
I take the shield of faith and quench all the fiery darts of the wicked.

Proverbs 3:7–8
I am not wise in my own eyes; I fear the LORD and depart from evil. This is health to my flesh and strength to my bones.

Proverbs 3:24
When I lie down, I will not be afraid; my sleep will be sweet

Proverbs 3:25
I am not afraid of sudden terror, nor of trouble from the wicked.

Proverbs 3:26 (AMP)
The Lord is my confidence, firm and strong. He will keep my foot from being caught in a trap.

Luke 1:38
May it be done to me according to Your word, Lord.

Luke 1:37
With God, *all* things are possible!

Psalms 118:17
I shall not die, but live, and declare the works of the LORD!

Luke 10:19
I have been given authority to tread on the enemy and nothing shall by any means hurt me!

Psalms 107:2
I am redeemed of the LORD, and I say so. He has delivered me out of the hand of the enemy.

Psalms 108:13
Through my God I shall do valiantly, for it is He who shall tread down my enemies.

John 14:13
Whatever I ask in Jesus' name, He will do!

Exodus 15:26
Jehovah Rapha is my healer.

Isaiah 33:24
And no one will say, "I am sick."

Isaiah 65:24
O LORD, before I ask, You will answer!

Exodus 15:26
You are the LORD who heals me.

Jeremiah 32:17
Nothing is too hard for You, Lord GOD.

Jeremiah 30:17
You will restore my health and heal my wounds.

Deuteronomy 7:15
You will remove every sickness, and I will not have any disease.

John 10:10 (NASU)
The thief comes only to steal and kill and destroy. You came that I may have life, and have it abundantly.

3 John 2
You desire that I prosper in all things and be in health, even as my soul prospers.

Isaiah 53:5
By Your stripes I am healed.

Psalms 103:3
You heal all my diseases.

Philippians 4:19
God, You supply all my needs according to Your riches in glory.

Psalms 84:11
No good thing will You withhold from me as I walk uprightly before You.

Proverbs 18:21
Death and life are in the power of the tongue, so I speak life over myself.

Psalms 89:34
Father, You will not violate your covenant, and You will not alter the words that have gone out of Your lips.

Hebrews 10:23 (KJV)
I will hold fast to my profession of faith, for You who have promised are faithful.

Deuteronomy 30:19
You have set before me life and death. I choose life!

2 Chronicles 20:15
The battle is not mine. It is God's.

Romans 8:37
In all things I am more than a conqueror.

Jeremiah 29:11
You have plans for me, plans for a [good] future and a hope.

Matthew 7:11
If I, being evil, know how to give good gifts to my children, how much more will You, heavenly Father, give good things to me when I ask.

Nehemiah 8:10
The joy of the LORD is my strength.

Hebrews 10:35
I refuse to throw away my confidence, because it will bring me great reward!

James 5:14–15
If anyone is sick among us, we call for the elders of the church, and they pray over the sick, anointing them with oil in the name of the Lord. And the prayer of faith will save the sick, and the Lord will raise them up. And if they have committed sins, they will be forgiven.

2 Corinthians 5:21; James 5:16 (KJV)
Because I am the righteousness of God in Christ Jesus, my effectual, fervent prayer avails much.

Proverbs 4:20–22
Father, I give attention to Your words. I incline my ears to Your sayings. I do not let them depart from my eyes. I keep them in the midst of my heart. For they are life to me and health to all my flesh.

Matthew 10:1
You have given me the power to heal all manner of diseases.

Mark 3:15
You gave me power to heal sickness.

Mark 16:17–18
According to God's Word, these signs follow me because I believe: In Jesus' name I cast out demons. I lay hands on the sick, and they recover.

1 Corinthians 12:9
Thank You, Lord, for giving me the gift of healing.

Luke 4:18
The Spirit of the LORD is upon me to heal the sick.

Romans 8:32
Father, You have freely given me all things.

Psalm 107:2
I am the redeemed of the LORD, and I say I'm healed and delivered out of all the hand of the enemy.

Mark 3:27
I bind the strongman who attempts to plunder my health.

Exodus 14:13
I will not be afraid. I will stand and see the salvation of the LORD.

Psalms 34:6
The LORD delivers me out of all my troubles.

Psalms 34:7
The angel of the LORD encamps around me and delivers me.

Psalms 34:8
I taste and see that the LORD is good!

Psalms 34:10
Because I seek the LORD, I shall not lack any good thing.

Proverbs 4:22
Father, Your words are life to me and health to all my flesh.

Psalms 55:22; 1 Peter 5:7
I cast all my burdens on You, LORD, because You care for me and will sustain me.

Mark 9:23
Because I believe, *all things* are possible.

Appendix B

HEALING SCRIPTURES

Genesis 20:17
So Abraham prayed to God; and God healed Abimelech, his wife, and his female servants. Then they bore children.

Exodus 15:26
"If you diligently heed the voice of the LORD your God and do what is right in His sight, give ear to His commandments and keep all His statutes, I will put none of the diseases on you which I have brought on the Egyptians. For I am the LORD who heals you."

Exodus 23:25
"So you shall serve the LORD your God, and He will bless your bread and your water. And I will take sickness away from the midst of you."

Deuteronomy 7:15
And the LORD will take away from you all sickness, and will afflict you with none of the terrible diseases of Egypt which you have known, but will lay them on all those who hate you.

Psalms 103:1–5
Bless the LORD, O my soul; and all that is within me, bless His holy name! Bless the LORD, O my soul, and forget not all His

THE POWER OF HOPE IN HOPELESS SITUATIONS

benefits: who forgives all your iniquities, who heals all your diseases, who redeems your life from destruction, who crowns you with lovingkindness and tender mercies, who satisfies your mouth with good things, so that your youth is renewed like the eagle's.

Psalms 107:20
He sent His word and healed them, and delivered them from their destructions.

Proverbs 3:5–8
Trust in the LORD with all your heart, and lean not on your own understanding; in all your ways acknowledge Him, and He shall direct your paths. Do not be wise in your own eyes; fear the LORD and depart from evil. It will be health to your flesh, and strength to your bones.

Proverbs 4:20–22
My son, give attention to my words; incline your ear to my sayings. Do not let them depart from your eyes; keep them in the midst of your heart; for they are life to those who find them, and health to all their flesh.

Isaiah 53:5
But He was wounded for our transgressions, He was bruised for our iniquities; the chastisement for our peace was upon Him, and by His stripes we are healed.

Isaiah 54:17
"No weapon formed against you shall prosper, and every tongue which rises against you in judgment you shall condemn. This is the heritage of the servants of the LORD, and their righteousness is from Me," says the LORD.

Isaiah 57:15, 18
For thus says the High and Lofty One Who inhabits eternity, whose name is Holy: "I dwell in the high and holy place, with him who has a contrite and humble spirit, to revive the spirit of the humble,

and to revive the heart of the contrite ones. . . . I have seen his ways, and will heal him; I will also lead him, and restore comforts to him and to his mourners."

Matthew 4:23
And Jesus went about all Galilee, teaching in their synagogues, preaching the gospel of the kingdom, and healing all kinds of sickness and all kinds of disease among the people.

Matthew 8:1–3
When He had come down from the mountain, great multitudes followed Him. And behold, a leper came and worshiped Him, saying, "Lord, if You are willing, You can make me clean."
Then Jesus put out His hand and touched him, saying, "I am willing; be cleansed." Immediately his leprosy was cleansed.

Matthew 8:14–15
Now when Jesus had come into Peter's house, He saw his wife's mother lying sick with a fever. So He touched her hand, and the fever left her. And she arose and served them.

Matthew 8:16–17
When evening had come, they brought to Him many who were demon-possessed. And He cast out the spirits with a word, and healed all who were sick, that it might be fulfilled which was spoken by Isaiah the prophet, saying: "He Himself took our infirmities and bore our sicknesses."

Matthew 12:15
But when Jesus knew it, He withdrew from there. And great multitudes followed Him, and He healed them all.

Matthew 15:30
Then great multitudes came to Him, having with them the lame, blind, mute, maimed, and many others; and they laid them down at Jesus' feet, and He healed them.

Matthew 21:14
Then the blind and the lame came to Him in the temple, and He healed them.

Mark 5:25–29
Now a certain woman had a flow of blood for twelve years, and had suffered many things from many physicians. She had spent all that she had and was no better, but rather grew worse. When she heard about Jesus, she came behind Him in the crowd and touched His garment. For she said, "If only I may touch His clothes, I shall be made well."
Immediately the fountain of her blood was dried up, and she felt in her body that she was healed of the affliction.

Mark 6:54–56
And when they came out of the boat, immediately the people recognized Him, ran through that whole surrounding region, and began to carry about on beds those who were sick to wherever they heard He was. Wherever He entered, into villages, cities, or in the country, they laid the sick in the marketplaces, and begged Him that they might just touch the hem of His garment. And as many as touched Him were made well.

Mark 7:32–35
Then they brought to Him one who was deaf and had an impediment in his speech, and they begged Him to put His hand on him. And He took him aside from the multitude, and put His fingers in his ears, and He spat and touched his tongue. Then, looking up to heaven, He sighed, and said to him, "Ephphatha," that is, "Be opened."
Immediately his ears were opened, and the impediment of his tongue was loosed, and he spoke plainly.

Mark 8:22–25
Then He came to Bethsaida; and they brought a blind man to Him, and begged Him to touch him. So He took the blind man by the

hand and led him out of the town. And when He had spit on his eyes and put His hands on him, He asked him if he saw anything. And he looked up and said, "I see men like trees, walking."
Then He put His hands on his eyes again and made him look up. And he was restored and saw everyone clearly.

Mark 16:17–18
"And these signs will follow those who believe: In My name they will cast out demons; they will speak with new tongues; they will take up serpents; and if they drink anything deadly, it will by no means hurt them; they will lay hands on the sick, and they will recover."

Luke 4:40
When the sun was setting, all those who had any that were sick with various diseases brought them to Him; and He laid His hands on every one of them and healed them.

Luke 5:15
However, the report went around concerning Him all the more; and great multitudes came together to hear, and to be healed by Him of their infirmities.

Luke 5:17
Now it happened on a certain day, as He was teaching, that there were Pharisees and teachers of the law sitting by, who had come out of every town of Galilee, Judea, and Jerusalem. And the power of the Lord was present to heal them.

Luke 6:6–10
Now it happened on another Sabbath, also, that He entered the synagogue and taught. And a man was there whose right hand was withered. So the scribes and Pharisees watched Him closely, whether He would heal on the Sabbath, that they might find an accusation against Him. But He knew their thoughts, and said to the man who had the withered hand, "Arise and stand here." And he arose and stood. Then Jesus said to them, "I will ask you one

thing: Is it lawful on the Sabbath to do good or to do evil, to save life or to destroy?" And when He had looked around at them all, He said to the man, "Stretch out your hand." And he did so, and his hand was restored as whole as the other.

Luke 6:19
And the whole multitude sought to touch Him, for power went out from Him and healed them all.

Luke 9:1–2
Then He called His twelve disciples together and gave them power and authority over all demons, and to cure diseases. He sent them to preach the kingdom of God and to heal the sick.

Luke 13:10–13
Now He was teaching in one of the synagogues on the Sabbath. And behold, there was a woman who had a spirit of infirmity eighteen years, and was bent over and could in no way raise herself up. But when Jesus saw her, He called her to Him and said to her, "Woman, you are loosed from your infirmity." And He laid His hands on her, and immediately she was made straight, and glorified God.

John 5:5–8
Now a certain man was there who had an infirmity thirty-eight years. When Jesus saw him lying there, and knew that he already had been in that condition a long time, He said to him, "Do you want to be made well?"
The sick man answered Him, "Sir, I have no man to put me into the pool when the water is stirred up; but while I am coming, another steps down before me."
Jesus said to him, "Rise, take up your bed and walk." And immediately the man was made well, took up his bed, and walked.
And that day was the Sabbath.

John 9:1–7

Now as Jesus passed by, He saw a man who was blind from birth. And His disciples asked Him, saying, "Rabbi, who sinned, this man or his parents, that he was born blind?"

Jesus answered, "Neither this man nor his parents sinned, but that the works of God should be revealed in him. I must work the works of Him who sent Me while it is day; the night is coming when no one can work. As long as I am in the world, I am the light of the world."

When He had said these things, He spat on the ground and made clay with the saliva; and He anointed the eyes of the blind man with the clay. And He said to him, "Go, wash in the pool of Siloam" (which is translated, Sent). So he went and washed, and came back seeing.

Acts 5:14–16

And believers were increasingly added to the Lord, multitudes of both men and women, so that they brought the sick out into the streets and laid them on beds and couches, that at least the shadow of Peter passing by might fall on some of them. Also a multitude gathered from the surrounding cities to Jerusalem, bringing sick people and those who were tormented by unclean spirits, and they were all healed.

Acts 9:32–34

Now it came to pass, as Peter went through all parts of the country, that he also came down to the saints who dwelt in Lydda. There he found a certain man named Aeneas, who had been bedridden eight years and was paralyzed. And Peter said to him, "Aeneas, Jesus the Christ heals you. Arise and make your bed." Then he arose immediately.

Acts 10:38

"How God anointed Jesus of Nazareth with the Holy Spirit and with power, who went about doing good and healing all who were oppressed by the devil, for God was with Him.

Acts 14:8–10

And in Lystra a certain man without strength in his feet was sitting, a cripple from his mother's womb, who had never walked. This man heard Paul speaking. Paul, observing him intently and seeing that he had faith to be healed, said with a loud voice, "Stand up straight on your feet!" And he leaped and walked.

Acts 28:8–9

And it happened that the father of Publius lay sick of a fever and dysentery. Paul went in to him and prayed, and he laid his hands on him and healed him. So when this was done, the rest of those on the island who had diseases also came and were healed.

Romans 8:11

But if the Spirit of Him who raised Jesus from the dead dwells in you, He who raised Christ from the dead will also give life to your mortal bodies through His Spirit who dwells in you.

1 Thessalonians 5:23

Now may the God of peace Himself sanctify you completely; and may your whole spirit, soul, and body be preserved blameless at the coming of our Lord Jesus Christ.

James 5:14–16

Is anyone among you sick? Let him call for the elders of the church, and let them pray over him, anointing him with oil in the name of the Lord. And the prayer of faith will save the sick, and the Lord will raise him up. And if he has committed sins, he will be forgiven. Confess your trespasses to one another, and pray for one another, that you may be healed. The effective, fervent prayer of a righteous man avails much.

1 Peter 2:24

Who Himself bore our sins in His own body on the tree, that we, having died to sins, might live for righteousness—by whose stripes you were healed.

3 John 2

Beloved, I pray that you may prosper in all things and be in health, just as your soul prospers.

CPSIA information can be obtained
at www.ICGtesting.com
Printed in the USA
BVOW09s1140120318
510355BV00002B/197/P